THE FOUR ESSENTIAL QUESTIONS

CHOOSING SPIRITUALLY HEALTHY HABITS

BECA LEWIS

PERCEPTION PUBLISHING

Contents

—•—

WHAT OTHERS SAY

WHAT OTHERS ARE SAYING ABOUT THE FOUR ESSENTIAL QUESTIONS
"Reading Beca Lewis is very much like sitting down for a quiet chat with a wise, close and trusted friend. In The Four Essential Questions Beca shares examples from her own life; her own experience; her own knowing, as she guides us to rediscover the Divine in all things and gently prompts us to examine who it is we truly are. Highly recommended."—Greg Willson, co-editor, Cultivate Life! Magazine

"Beca Lewis makes heaven feel so down to earth! Her writing is clearly inspired, yet practical, provable, and proven by her as evidenced through the wise yet humble stories she tells about her own experiences. The Four Essential Questions definitely helped to open my eyes to some unseen limits I may have been accepting for myself or in denial about, and at the same time brought a sigh of relief that I could be free of them!

Her message comes with honesty and conviction, yet no preachiness or judgment. The book feels just like a warm and ongoing conversation she has been having with God, which we have been made welcome to sit in on. Very comforting, inspiring, and FUN to read! I would highly recommend this book to fellow seekers and I know I'll be reading it again!"—Laura Moliter, CS, Author of The Key to the Kingdom: How a Change in Perspective Can Make Your Earth More Like Heaven and the e-book, Inspiration and Exultation: Healing Ideas for Every Day

"Beca Lewis has written a thoughtful and deeply felt spiritual guide to dissolving the material habits that keep us from our spiritual nature. It is a calming meditation that will help you move through the daily cacophony to a place of deep inner peace and love. Bravo, Beca! Thank you for this." —Chellie Campbell, author of *The Wealthy Spirit and Zero to Zillionaire*

"You put a wonderful book together. I loved how you organized it, how you positioned the profound with the concrete, and your honesty. I haven't seen a book quite like this, Beca. I stayed up late to finish it. It was unput-downable. I really, really loved this book!"—Gloria Wendroff, Godwriter, author of *Heavenletters, Love Letters from God,* Winner of Chelson 2004 Inspiration Book Award

DEDICATION

To my husband, Delbert Lee Piper, Sr., whose inspiration, feedback, support, and love have made all the difference, and whose influence is seen everywhere in my life, including in this book.

— · —

FORWARD

U se this book as a handy life guide.

I think of a guide as something, or someone, that keeps us aiming in the direction we want to be going. A guide has traveled ahead of us and has seen the dangers and the glories of the road that lies ahead.

Knowing where we want to go, it keeps us on track, and leads us away from danger, so we can enjoy the journey and arrive safely at our destination.

Sometimes a guide can do that gently. A simple whisper and a soft nudge is enough. Other times a yank on the arm or a shove in the back is necessary to keep us from falling off the cliff towards which we are blindly walking.

For a guide to be effective, we must be truthful to it. If we lie to the guide about what we want, who we are, and where we are going, we will end up in the wrong place.

As you read this book, tell the truth to yourself.

Use these questions to readjust the direction you are traveling based on what you learn.

Let *The Four Essential Questions* become your personal guide so that you remain safely on the path to your destination.

PREFACE

*H*abit with him was all the test of truth. It must be right: I've done it from my youth. —George Crabbe

We all have habits—some of them work in our favor. However, the ones that are formed through unknown and unconscious perceptions always work against us without our knowledge. In order to eliminate these dangerous habits, and replace them with spiritually healthy habits, we have to drill down into our thinking and perceptions.

We will use *The Four Essential Questions* as the drill. Once the way is cleared, we can consciously choose the habits that work for us; not against us. In this book, you will find the tools you need to continue to check, and eliminate, the habits that are no longer wanted, and build spiritually healthy ones.

When drilling into a deep piece of wood, it is necessary to continually pull the drill-bit out so the sawdust created lifts out of the hole.

Otherwise, the sawdust compacts and makes it harder and harder to drill. On the other hand, when we keep on drilling, and clearing out, at the end, the drill bit breaks through, and the last of the sawdust falls through easily. The hole is clear and ready to be used.

If we don't completely drill the hole the whole way through there are two results. The obvious one is that it was a waste of time to do all that drilling because without a completed hole nothing can be done with it. The other, not so obvious, is that the hole will, over time, fill up with "stuff."

This also happens when we dig a hole for a plant. Of course, we know that the dirt must be taken out of the hole, in order to be even called a hole. However, if we don't fill the hole with the intended plant, it will eventually fill up with something else.

We dug plant holes one year expecting to plant trees, but never got around to it. The next year, the holes had to be completely cleared again in order to be ready for the trees.

This same idea happens with ruts. My husband Del sees this all the time when working in the woods. If a machine has gone through and caused ruts, and they were not filled in again with soil, eventually they fill up on their own.

Perhaps this seems okay, but it isn't really, because they don't fill up with solid dirt. Instead, they fill with loose things like leaves and grass. This makes them invisible to someone using the path or road, and causes a dangerous hazard for anyone who steps, or drives, into them.

This is the same with uncovering habits. We are really drilling down into our thinking, but if we don't go the whole way through, the empty space will simply fill up with unwanted, and unknown, "stuff."

That is why it is important in drilling down into our perceptions to continue the process of clearing unwanted habits. If we experience a small amount of freedom, or life changes a bit for the better, it will be tempting to simply stop and go no further. However, if we stop before completion, then like the uncompleted hole in the wood, the unplanted hole in the dirt, or the unfilled rut, we have an even worse situation than we had before.

Sometimes holes are easy to drill, dig, and fill in. Other times they are not. However, if the going sometimes seems to be too hard, or even boring, because it isn't happening fast enough, keep going anyway. Use the questions in this book to help you through it; to make it easier and even to make it fun.

The reward is far greater than the apparent effort.

Just as when we finish drilling a hole and the last of the sawdust simply drops out, if we keep on going, the last of the unwanted perceptions that have caused the habit will simply drop away.

There are only two mistakes one can make along the road to truth: not going all the way, and not starting. — Buddha

1

— · —

CHAPTER ONE

A human being is part of a whole, called by us the "universe," a part limited in time and space. He experiences himself, his thoughts and feelings, as something separate from the rest—a kind of optical delusion of his consciousness. This delusion is a kind of prison for us, restricting us to our personal desires and to affection for a few persons nearest us. Our task must be to free ourselves from this prison by widening our circles of compassion to embrace all living creatures and the whole of nature in its beauty. —Albert Einstein

Since we were very young, inside all of our heads, a voice suggests something to each of us. That suggestion is usually in the form of a question, which is why I call it a *life question*. We are rarely aware of our life question, and since we are unaware of it, it runs our life, because of the perception it creates.

Seneca Elder, Twylah Nitche, said, *If you are not getting the right answers, you are not asking the right questions.* Obviously, we must discover our own personal life question and break its pattern in order to live the life we want to live and to be free of its grasp.

To discover our life question, we have to listen, and observe, our own conversations, and our own life. Once we discover it, the next step is learn how to face and replace it with a statement that works for us, not against us.

We see the results of these life questions when we begin to notice that life isn't working as well as we know it could work, and that the path we are on is not taking us where we thought we wanted to go.

The good news is, there are only a few of these life questions, and we all say, or ask them, with a variation or two.

Perhaps yours is like one of these:

- I don't know.
- Why do I have to live up to everyone's expectations?
- Why is life so hard?
- Why is life so unfair?
- Why am I this way?

It is possible that you don't recognize these questions for yourself immediately, but if you listen to your external and internal conversations, you will begin to hear, and recognize, the one that you have been saying and asking all your life. This question, or statement, is currently the guide of your life.

Do you really want to be guided by the perceptions, "I don't know, Why do I have to live up to everyone's expectations, Why is life so hard, Why is life so unfair, Why am I this way?" Of course not!

The Four Essential Questions we will ask in this book will break the pattern of that life question which is really a life-sentence. Breaking that pattern is the key to living the life that we want to live, were meant to live, and desire to live; not sometime in the future, but here and now.

Of course, we all know the definition of insanity as spoken by Albert Einstein: Doing the same thing over and over again and expecting different results.

Ask these *Four Essential Questions* and answer them truthfully, and you can absolutely expect different results!

PERCEPTION RULES

What we perceive to be reality magnifies.—Beca Lewis

In the world of marketing, one is supposed to come up with a "catch phrase" or USP (unique selling proposition). Many, many, years ago I condensed all that I was trying to say into this phrase: What We Perceive To Be Reality Magnifies.

Years later, I am still using it because it is the clearest way to explain that what appears as reality—is not. Perception is reality. This is different from what is meant by the saying, "What we focus upon creates reality," which implies that we are creators or at least co-creators. It's easier than that, because perception is reality. However, the big question is—whose perception, and can we shift ours and thereby shift what appears as our world? The answer is "yes," but first we need to know and understand how perception works, or rules.

On the TV program *60 Minutes*, a General spoke about war as a perception. While working as a Certified Financial Planner, I learned that the stock market is an agreed-upon perception. The worldview that governs so much of our lives, is an agreed-upon perception. Everything that the five senses tell us is a perception—not a real thing, but a perception. Nevertheless, these kinds of perceptions block from view what is big R Reality.

Cleaning up perception is not creating a new world. It is seeing the world as it really is, completely and irresistibly, perfectly spiritual.

Then what is spiritual? Is it a cleaned-up material view that attracts what we want to us, and creates a perfect lifestyle? Is it measurable energy that can be manipulated and used to benefit us?

No, that is a material perception. Spiritual, Spirit, is not measurable. Spiritual is not measurable by the human senses. It is not related to dogmas or human opinions. It is the seven nouns of God in action—Soul, Mind, Spirit, Love, Life, Principle, and Truth*. It is the logic behind it all. It is the essence and power of unconditional Intelligent Love.

As we become aware of the thoughts, ideas, beliefs, and perceptions that color the world we see, we can choose whether we want to continue with the limited, chaotic, often cruel, and never fixable perception of the worldview, or the elegant, logical, entirely loving, always supportive, One Intelligent Mind, God's perception.

Since what we perceive to be reality magnifies, why not choose to magnify what God sees and knows? That perception is the perfect one, containing all that is, holding every element of Its idea called world, man, universe, animals, plants, every blade of grass, and every grain of sand as Itself in action.

The proof that there is a God, is that you and I, and all that we know, exists. All questions about why and how are distractions. If our intent is to know as God knows, then let's forget the human questions; and instead practice seeing as God sees.

Of course, this involves discovering, uncovering, eliminating, dissolving, and letting go of all perceptions that block our sight to the One Perceiver. Assuming we are all willing to do this, because our intent is to see as God sees, then the next step is to become aware of what we believe to be reality and see if it is in alignment with the Truth of One Cause and Creator.

This is not a judgment time; this is simply an awareness of the misperceptions that we have held dear. This is what will result in a life shift.

This is doing dirt-time and deep practicing. As we make that shift, and awareness begins to creep into our life, lots of "stuff" appears that is not necessarily what we wanted, or expected, to see.

It's like moving. As we take things out of closets and drawers and decide if we want to move it to the next place, or throw it away, we are amazed to find that we have not paid attention to what has been accumulating in our home.

It's the same with a state of mind. We hide past actions, hurts, and sorrows in boxes, and drawers, and closets in our mind. As we move from the past state of mind to the next one, we get to decide what to take with us and what to discard.

When we move from a physical home, we touch physical objects to make the decision about what to keep.

If we get emotional about why we have it, thinking that it can't be replaced, get mad at ourselves for not noticing it before, or practice any other form of judgment, then we can be stuck in that moving process forever. It's not necessary to do this.

In the same way, as we examine our perceptions, ideas, and beliefs that we have accumulated, it is not necessary to understand the why and how of each one.

It is not necessary to beat ourselves up for the mistaken points of view that have lived in our thoughts. If we did this, we would never move. That point of view would be our mental home for a long time.

What we can do instead is choose whether the object in our home, or the perception in our thought, is how we want to live now. We can let go of anything that isn't the highest understanding we currently have of the perfection of Love.

As we clean our home, what has always been there becomes visible. As we clean our perception, what has always been present becomes visible.

If the doors of perception were cleansed everything would appear to man as it is, infinite. For man has closed himself up, till he sees all things thru' narrow chinks of his cavern. —William Blake

Let's stop trying to perceive what is real through the narrow chinks of our cavern. Let's choose to see as God sees—Infinitely. Then there is no need for a secret on how to create and achieve, because it will be clear to us that all we need is already present, and all that needs to be done has already been completed, in big R Reality.

Yes, perception rules.

There is no getting away from it. It is like the ever-present air that we breathe, or the force that keeps us from floating off the planet. It exists as a law, so it is best to make friends with it, understand it, and learn how to use it for good, and in this way the habits we form will be from this new perception. The results are almost unimaginable.

*Synonyms of God as stated by Mary Baker Eddy

Two Modes Of Perception

The only real voyage of discovery consists not in seeking new landscapes but in having new eyes.—Marcel Proust

We know now that *what we perceive to be reality magnifies.* Perception is our reality. What we believe and perceive within, is what is seen without.

There are two modes of perception: *state of mind and point of view.* We get to choose both; this is the meaning of free will. Our choices do not change big R Reality, they simply allow us to see and experience more or less of it in our daily lives.

To live congruently, our point of view perception and state of mind perception must be in sync and harmony. This is much harder to do, than to say.

This is why an unknown life question can be so devastating to our life. It means that without our awareness, it has created a point of view that builds the life we are experiencing, which in turn builds an unhealthy habit. Dissolving that question through awareness, we can consciously choose our own point of view and corresponding state of mind.

It is important to know that I am not talking about positive thinking, or even mind over matter. Both of these ideas exist in the small limited realm, or small r reality, and only work by using human will power, or human strength. I am talking about letting go of the illusion, the misperception, of humanness, and stepping into the unstoppable force called Love, or Mind, or God.

Perhaps you don't care to access this Infinite realm. So be it for now. It doesn't really matter at this time, because all I am asking you to understand and accept is that perception is reality, and as we shift ours, the world shifts with us.

THREE HABIT STORIES

Story One:
For over 6 years, I had eaten peanuts in the shell for breakfast. This may be a crazy breakfast, but I loved it all the same. However, every time I cracked a peanut, little peanut pieces flew around which required some careful cleanup afterward. Then one day Del decided this was the day I could learn the

easy way to eat peanuts. Instead of breaking them in half I just had to look, or feel, for the dimple in the top of the peanut, give a slight push and the peanut opened easily, with very little flinging of pieces.

I was amazed to learn I had been cracking peanuts the hard way for years. However, that was the easiest part of the lesson. Ever since then I have to remind myself constantly, "Not that way," as I crack instead of push, "this way." I am still working on eating peanuts the easy way.

Story Two:

When we used to go to an office, some mornings we had to use a swipe card to get in before the doors were officially unlocked. The office had three doors, two of which are right beside each other. One day, another person and I reached the two doors at the same time.

I swiped my card in the one door as he swiped his in the other. As I did so, he turned to me and said, "What? This card works on that door too?"

He had worked in that office for almost two years and had taken the longer route to his office all that time because, obviously, the first person who had shown him how to use the card showed him how to open the side door. For two years, he had never thought to try the card in the other door, or even noticed that other people entered through different doors.

Story Three:

We had two cars, therefore two huge car keys to carry around on our key chains. I had taken one set of keys off my chain since I never used the other car. I kept the keys in a bowl by the door.

Then one day we decided that I best put the keys back on the chain. I looked in the bowl and they weren't there.

I remembered that I had thought of taking the one set with us when we were traveling and I decided that I must not have returned it to the bowl afterwards. I searched our traveling stuff and it wasn't there. For the next few months, every time I thought about it I would look for the keys. In the car I would look under the seats, in the glove compartments, in desk drawers—anywhere I thought I might have put them.

One day, Del decided to take the Thule off the top of one of the cars. He went to the box where we keep keys that we rarely use to get those specific keys and—yes— you guessed it, there were my car keys. I remember that when I was cleaning months before, I had put the keys in the box for rarely used keys.

Why didn't I look there? Because, as soon as I realized they weren't in the bowl I assumed that I had not returned the keys to their proper place after traveling, because I had accepted that I am a person that misplaces keys.

Imagine what would have happened if I would have said to myself instead, "There is only One Mind and that Mind is intelligent and never misplaces anything. Therefore, this mistaken belief about myself is not true and cannot affect my world."

Changing patterns, or habits we don't want to keep, to the spiritually healthy habits that we want, takes five steps:

- It must occur to us that there is another (and easier) way.
- We must be willing to learn this new way.
- We have to learn the new way.

- We have to actually do the new way
- We have to remember that we learned it!

This is what we will do together in this book: learn, practice, and remember that we learned how!

2

— · —

Chapter Two

I *cannot imagine a God who rewards and punishes the objects of his creation, whose purposes are modeled after our own—a God, in short, who is but a reflection of human frailty.*—Albert Einstein

Hasn't everyone wondered, at least once, how God could allow the suffering, death, and intentional evil in the world to exist? How could he let wars continue? How can he be on both sides of a controversy?

Of course, we have also looked at the other side. We have observed the harmony and beauty of a flower, the flight of a bird, the majesty of a mountain, and we have wondered where all that could have come from, if not from an Infinite Intelligence.

In the long-standing debate over "is there a God" or "isn't there a God," we can agree with both sides.

The answer is: "no," there isn't a God that allows evil to exist; and "yes," there is a God that is the Principle of Life.

Perhaps part of the problem is the word God. Depending on what framework of perception we grew up within, and have worked out for ourselves, either we love this name of God, or we hate it.

If we could drop our preconceived ideas about what the word God means, perhaps we would find that we are all in agreement. Perhaps we would also find a way to resolve our own internal struggle with why evil appears to exist if God is Love.

What if we stopped seeing God in terms of a powerful human that knows both good and evil, and can be swayed by human prayer and opinion?

What if instead we saw God through a scientific and Spiritual Perception as the Mind Fabric of what we perceive as the Infinite Universe?

What if God were The Infinite Intelligence that both creates and holds it all together? What if God is not in any way human, but instead is like the principle of math, the Principle of Life?

Don't most of us blithely say that God is omnipresent, omniscience, omnipotent, and omniaction? Have we stopped to examine what this means and implies? Isn't this a scientific statement that leads us to the evidence of God as the Principle of Life?

Could this God, the Principle of Life, be both good and evil? Wouldn't this idea of duality negate omni? There can be no debate. Either God is completely good, or God is completely evil.

The original meaning of the word God is Good. Makes sense doesn't it? Because if God is evil, it stands to reason that eventually, it would destroy itself. Therefore, thinking logically, there cannot be a God that knows evil, or is on both sides of a controversy. There can only be a God that is the Infinite Principle of Life.

However, what about what we experience as evil, lack, sorrow, and ill health? All these are present in the worldview, the human god's world, but not in the big R Reality that is the Principle of Life, all moving in perfect harmony. Anything that doesn't appear as Good is a distortion of Truth.

Here's where we exercise what we call our free will. **We choose**. And our choice determines our experience. We can't be on both sides of the fence, or serve two masters. We get to choose the perception of Infinite Good,—and when we choose and live this perception, and make it the basis of our thought and actions, then what isn't true will dissolve, revealing what Is.

Much evil is done in God's name. However, that doesn't make it God's fault. When we interpret God as if It were human, this assumption will inevitably lead to both good and bad consequences. One side will win and one side will lose.

We can always tell when we are living from the human god idea. We start working hard at fixing things, making things better, being right, getting healthy, getting rich, or just getting by.

Our thoughts are filled with either worry, or competition. The human god starts with duality, and knows both good and evil. Everyone knows what the results of this looks like in our lives, and in the world. It's not God that lets evil exist. We let it exist in the only place possible, in our acceptance of duality and a human god. It only exists in the same way that darkness exists before we turn on the light.

Again, the answer is "no," there is no God that knows good and evil, and "yes," there is a God that is omniscient Good.

The more we begin with this Truth and live in it, the more we make it the premise of our being, and the more it will dissolve anything that is blocking the view of the unlimited good and abundance of the omnipresent Infinite One.

When we make this choice, we will experience our own personal evidence of the existence of God as All.

So make up any name you want to for God, because God by any name is still All There Is, and It is Infinite Intelligent Good.

CONCENTRIC CIRCLES OF LOVE

Love is the only currency that can never be devalued. We only need to share and receive it freely.—Beca Lewis

The great artist Van Gogh said to his brother Theo, "I tell you, the more I think, the more I feel that there is nothing more truly artistic than to love people." I wonder if Van Gogh would mind if I took away the word *people* so that his sentence would simply end with the word *love*.

Wouldn't this expand the picture? Instead of thinking that we can only love those people, places, and things that look exactly like us, we could expand the idea of love to include everyone and everything.

As I write this, on our dining table is a dish with rocks and water in it. Sitting on top of those rocks and water, are some blooming narcissus bulbs. Every time I look at them, I marvel at their beauty and their promise that spring isn't that far away.

It is a concentric circle of love.

The dish by itself would have been empty and fairly boring. Filled with rocks and water, it still would have not been much to look at. Add the bulbs to the dish, rocks, and water, and they now all have a purpose. At the same time, without the rocks, water, and dish the bulbs would not be blooming.

This is an example of how that concentric circle of love supports and expands. As we see the flowers, we are filled with joy at their beauty, and we pass on those lovely spring feelings to each other, and then to another, and another, and another.

We are all like a stone thrown into the water, concentric circles expanding to include, and touch everything.

Recently I saw a video of a crow that loved and cared for a kitten who could have died without him; and the kitten reciprocated by loving him back. This love continued even after the kitten turned into a cat and found a home. Each morning the crow waited for him by the door, until he came out to play.

What if the crow would have looked at the kitten and thought, "He doesn't look like me, and don't cats normally kill birds?" Instead, he showed love and got love back, and that shared love has been a continuing expanding circle to everyone who sees and hears about it.

One Christmas, my husband gave me a whole pack of DVDs that he called "happy movies" because each of them ends with *love*. One of the movies is called, "Stardust." In this movie, the heroine shows the hero that true love does not need proof of its love. It doesn't require sacrifice and sorrow. It doesn't love for prestige. As they lived this truth, the world they found themselves in transformed.

In another movie "Enchanted," the heroine is so infused with love that her point of view expands into, and through, everyone and everything she meets. She shifts the world into which she was un-lovingly banished. Without blame, and by being only love, she too transforms that world around her.

Concentric circles of love. We are all at the center, and the cause, of concentric circles.

We get to choose whether that circle will be one of love, or of the multitude of other names for what is not love. The opposite of love hides behind words like sorrow, blame, despair, upset, anger, or revenge, but it is always just the opposite of love, and only has power because we choose it instead of love. That concentric circle does not end well—for anyone.

In order to be a concentric circle of love we have to start with the love of ourselves. Starting there it is easy to be a stone of love that begins the circle of love that expands to transform the world.

Like the crow that loved the kitten, we have to begin by being happy with ourselves, content with who we are. We love by not looking at what we don't have (how does a crow feed or hug a kitten?), but by what we **do** have. We have the capacity to love because that is the essence of our being.

None of us can do anything alone. Like the flowers in the dish, we must have each other's support and encouragement. Without each other, we will feel empty and unfulfilled. Try as we might we cannot stop the concentric circle that extends from what we do and say. It is our choice whether we expand love, or the opposite of love.

As we choose love, that concentric circle will bring into each of our lives the fullness of what it means to love and be loved, and together we can enjoy the sweet fragrance of each of our unique blooms.

It doesn't matter if we are the cat or the crow. The crow had to give love to something he wasn't supposed to love, and in return, the cat had to accept love from something he wasn't supposed to trust. If they can do it, we can too! Like the women in "Enchanted" and "Stardust" we can transform the world we were "sent to" into the world we know it really is—Love in action.

STEP INTO THE GOOD

When love and skill work together, expect a masterpiece.—John Ruskin

Our garage was stuffed full! We had just moved and the building that would house Del's workshop wasn't ready yet. So we had moved all of his work equipment into the tiny garage, plus the things that we hadn't found a place for yet in the house.

It was so full I couldn't find anything, so Del arranged it enough to get an overview of what was there.

It was better and we were grateful, but I knew Del longed to be able to get to his equipment easier.

Later that day, two of our kids came over and asked if they could help with anything. "Yes," I said, and pointed to the garage. "Can you make it any better?" A few hours later, they had the garage completely clear in the middle, with everything in order all around the sides. I stared speechless for many minutes. It was amazing and completely unexpected.

In anticipation of Del seeing the garage, we all ran out to meet him as he drove up in his truck. "Look," I said as I pointed to the garage. No reaction. He backed up right to it with all three of us pointing and saying, "Look."

He looked, but had no real reaction. He got out of the truck and looked in; still no reaction; then he walked into the garage and saw it.

He stood in the middle of all that good, as speechless as I had been. In his mind, there had been no way it could have looked like that, so no matter how many times we pointed, he had to get out and actually walk into it to see how amazingly good it had become.

It was a perception, a preconceived perception. We all have them. Things can only be so good, can only look a specific way, and can only come to us in a particular way. It's a locked-in paradigm in our own minds.

Good could be sitting beside us, chatting us up, and we would miss it if we didn't know enough to walk in and look.

However, how do we look for good when we have no idea what good to look for?

Actually what we need to do is step into good, and then we'll see it. Here's an example how that looked to me on a speaking trip.

While waiting for the plane, I was contemplating how much I had recently let human perception become my focus rather than Spiritual Perception.

With nothing much else to do, I decided it was as good a time as any to start practicing Spiritual Perception with more diligence.

I took the phrase, *Since God is One and All, everything that is present is present as God only,** and started practicing what that means. I continued practicing Spiritual Perception, which is seeing good, or God, in place of what the five senses report. I looked at the people around me, and tried my best to see through what looked like people and see the qualities of God.

I looked at my chair, my computer, the ticket in my hand, and tried to see the qualities of God. I saw beauty, kindness, order, practicality, safety, and comfort. After just a few minutes of doing this, I heard my name called to come to the ticket counter, where I was told that I had been reassigned to a business class seat, so that a family could fly together.

I hadn't been practicing Spiritual Perception to get something. However, as I practiced, I stepped into the good, and the outcome was something that made my trip much more pleasant.

There is one more part to this story.

After getting the upgrade, I had to calm down my personal sense by reminding myself that I wasn't practicing to get, but to understand. So I continued looking through what appeared to be a person, place, or thing, and attempted to see God instead. As we were all lined up to board, I heard two men talk about how hard this flight was going to be for them. I didn't hear why, but I did have the fleeting thought that it didn't have to be that way.

Within moments, the same ticket guy called their names and handed them both upgrades. Spiritual Perception was revealing good for all, which of course is the way it is, since God is One and All. Spiritual Perception reveals that there is nothing going on but God, Good.

Instead of thinking that there will be a time that the tares will be separated from the wheat, we know that as we gain spiritual awareness, what appears to be tares are not something that must be destroyed, but simply wheat misperceived, and then that misperception will completely dissolve what appears to be tares.

Step into the good by practicing Spiritual Perception, and reap the benefit of the constant ever-providing harvest of the Infinite.

This is a practice that will benefit everyone. It doesn't take special equipment, or the perfect time, or money, or personal ability. It is available to each one of us at all times

We can begin now, and never stop stepping into the good, by practicing Spiritual Perception in each moment.

*John Hargreaves—*The Indivisibility Of The Infinite*

Right Thinking

The smallest fact is a window through which the infinite may be seen.—Aldous Huxley

Since it is a law that perception rules, and what we perceive to be reality magnifies, the most important thing we can do is to learn how to think rightly, or practice right thinking. There are seven steps to right thinking. Practice these correctly every day, and you will marvel at how fast life will change for the better for you.

Following these seven steps is the perfect way to start your day, or to heal any situation. I have used some personal examples to get you started.

Step One: Set Your Right Intent

This Book Intent: To give you clear and easy tools that you can use to discover and eliminate useless, destructive perceptions, and in doing so reveal your and Unique Spiritual Blessing.

My Personal Intent: To be more loving in every area of my life.

What is your Intent?

Step Two: State Your Right Premise

27

This Book Premise: There is only One Infinite Power, and it is Good.

Accepting this premise doesn't mean we have to believe or understand it at first. We simply have to accept it, and let ourselves move to an increasingly clearer understanding of it.

There are many names for this power; many of us call It God. Mind, Soul, Principle, Life, Truth, Love, and Spirit are also names for this One Infinite power. Because this One is omnipresent, omniscient, omniaction, and omnipotent, there is no room for any other power. This One's power is rooted in, based on, and operates from, the Principle of Intelligent Love.

This One is spiritual. We misperceive people, places, and things as material, or grounded and created in matter, when actually they are the ideas and reflection of the consciousness of the One power, or Mind.

This means that what we perceive as matter, and a material universe, is a misperception of a spiritual universe. There are not two universes, just one: God's.

As we begin this journey together, we are going to make this premise our starting point. Instead of thinking of ourselves as humans with imperfections, let's begin with the premise that within the truth of big R Reality we are much more: we are the idea of God and Its glorious reflection.

Let's begin with the premise that we are perfect now, and we have only to uncover and dissolve our misperceptions to live in the happiness and harmony that is already present. This book isn't about why this is true. This book is based on that fact.

Let's relax into the Truth that we are not what appears to our five senses, and we are not what we have been trained to believe, within the small r reality.

We are much more; we are the idea and action of the One Infinite Divine Intelligence. It doesn't matter what name you use for this Intelligence, it is still, and always, the Principle of Love.

My Personal Premise: God is Love and fills all space, and is visible to us in what appears as people, places, and things.

What Is Your Premise?

Step Three: State Your Right Identity

My Personal Right Identity: I am the action of Love.

It's actually easy to say, or state, a spiritual premise, but harder to place ourselves within it. As we step onto this spiritual path and take on the right perception of ourselves, we also must relieve ourselves of any guilt, judgment, and story that may want to attach itself to us.

Remind yourself that you are the Light of Love, and everything you discover on this journey is either leading you to that awareness, or has been trying to hide it from you.

We are letting go of what we don't want, and embracing what we do want. Laying down our ego and taking up the Truth of our Being is a joyous event, and one we can share together.

Instead of justifying why we think we are human, let's rejoice in the fact that we are more than that, and embrace what we perceive as human within the arms of Infinite Good. This way, in our everyday life, we are not questioning how we are doing humanly; instead, we are glorifying God in the way that we live.

What Is Your Right Identity?

We have laid the foundation of our perception. We have stated a right intent, premise, and identity. Now we come to the "work."

Step Four: Right Resistance

When we declare the Truth, both of God and our being, what is not true becomes more visible and often much noisier.

Since we are making a break away from ideas that have blinded us from the Truth, that lie will begin a campaign to change our minds.

Everything that we have ever heard within our head will get louder. It will try to dissuade us from our intention, premise, and identity.

One suggestion that it will make is that if we are spiritual and perfect now, that negates our human experience.

The suggestion will come to us that all that we experience within our lives is a lie, and if we fully accept the premise of One power now, all the good we see, and all the good we do does not mean anything.

The lie will remind us that we seem to experience two powers. One is the power of Love, or God, and the other is the power of evil, or the devil. Both appear to exist here in the place we perceive as separated from the Infinite One. We call this place the universe, or more locally, the earth.

The Bible records these two powers in the two stories of creation. In the first story, God, within Its consciousness creates (knows) everything, and it is Good. In the second story the but appears out of the mist and presents a second power and life where both good and evil are known.

Most of our daily lives are lived within the context of the second but story and all that stems from knowing, and accepting, both good and evil. Within the second story, most of us attempt to be good humans—and we succeed, some of the time. However, we are always confronted with, and confounded, by that belief in another power other than Good.

Instead of resisting the Truth, which is the intention of the lie, we must resist the lie. One very powerful way to do that is to use right reasoning to reason our way back to Truth.

Step Five: Right Reasoning

Let's reason rightly with the lie that says that if we start with the premise of only One power which is infinite, Intelligent Good, we negate our human experience. Beginning with the premise that there is only one power, does not negate what appears as a human experience.

Why? Because there is not a material and a spiritual universe, there is only a spiritual one. All that is present is present as God only. Our life, the world, the universe seen as two places, with two powers, is not so much an illusion as a misunderstanding.

31

God could not know about a misconception of Itself. It is Infinite, omnipresent Good. Where is the place It knows about evil or even shades of good? Obviously, it is nowhere.

The fact that the Infinite is All-Good does not mean we don't provide comfort, food, shelter, love, and care for ourselves and each other. On the contrary, in doing so we are demonstrating the Truth that Good is omnipresent, seen in these moments as "us" in action, as Love Loving Itself.

We do not have to live with the *but* story. Instead, we can say the word *and* which will take us to the first story of perfection.

When we acknowledge the omnipotence, omnipresence, omniaction, and omniscience of God we can say, "And that means my daily life is within that context.

As I understand, live, work with, and practice this premise, the mist rises and dissolves revealing what I have perceived of a human life as Life, God, expressed and lived as me."

We can embrace the and, and release the but.

It is our awareness of the omnipresence of Good that shines through our misunderstanding of what we perceive as a human life that results in what appears as an improved human condition. It is our confusion and misunderstanding that blocks the continual awareness of continual Good. We do not cause it, we do not create it; we are only temporarily blinded by it.

The river of Good is constant. The shining of Good is omnipresent. Accepting this premise brings a sigh of relief. It is the path of freedom. It does not take away, or create, what is real, but reveals it.

If we say, "It's all an illusion" and use that as an excuse to not participate fully in life, we are in error. It helps to say instead, "This is a misperception of what is really present and going on," and know that all action we take within our highest understanding of God is God Itself in action.

This way of thinking dissolves the boundaries between us, and lifts the confusion.

We can look at both the theories of evolution and intelligent design, and see that the Truth resides in both. Instead of fighting for a human way of life that lives with two powers, we can live as we are: One.

Instead of separation, comparison and judgment we find the intimacy of One—and our eternal and distinct spiritual identity is revealed.

Step Six: Right Practice

Ask yourself this question as we reveal your true spiritual identity and as you practice this shift, "What are the possibilities, and where is my focus?"

It takes deep spiritual practice, and using what we know, in order to grow. We can't attend to it in just an hour or two a week and hope that we will understand, and that things will change.

Spiritual Perception is a moment-by-moment decision to be aware of the Truth, or essence of Life, and to dissolve any lie claiming anything but Good is always present.

Step Seven: Right Action

Do we have to give up something to experience this? Yes we do. We have to give up the ego that protects the but story.

This is easy to do when we realize that we are not giving up the essence of ourselves, and that it is not negating our life; it is validating it. Selling all for the pearl of great price is what we are doing.

Releasing our beliefs that may have served us well in the past, but are no longer needed, is not a sacrifice, it is a gift.

When we experience joy and love, we are experiencing Truth breaking through our fog of misperceptions, just as the sun breaks through the clouds. It is always present; all we have to do is shift our perception, and let go of what blinds us to the presence of Love.

3

– • –

Chapter Three

I slept and dreamt that life was joy. I awoke and saw that life was service. I acted and behold, service was joy. —Rabindranath Tagore

She was always-on-call. I wanted to be like her, but I had no idea how I could handle what she did with such apparent ease. Any time of the day or night, any time of the year, she was always on call for those that needed comfort, or understanding, and yes, healing.

I remember the time that I called her in the middle of the night because my baby was having convulsions, and I knew I could turn to her. I was hysterical. She answered the phone with no tiredness in her voice, present and available. She told me the Truth about my child. She reminded me that my little girl was in Reality the child of God, was Light itself, and that there was no room for anything else. I calmed down, and within minutes so did my child, the child of Light. It was over and never returned.

Always-on-call, how did she do it? Thinking I was not capable of this feat of love, I chose other ways to live. I thought about "disappearing" where no one could find me or need me. I tried not to influence people in case I did something wrong that hurt them forever. I disappeared into my busy work, my business, and sometimes my sorrow.

I knew my friend had things to think through, and I felt privileged to be someone she spoke to when she wanted to share. We had lunch together and talked about our kids and her grandchildren. I organized her papers, I knew what she needed to resolve. However, through all that, she was always present and on call for others no matter when, or where, the need appeared.

Eventually, I realized that we are all always-on-call, whether we want to be or not. We can run, we can hide, we can lie, and we can wait, but none of these actions will take away the fact that we are always on call—because that is a function of being alive. The question is—are we on call in a way that pleases us and brings happiness, or on call in a way that constricts and imprisons us?

Did I tell you that I never knew her not to be happy? Always-on-call, and always happy is a way of life that all of us can achieve.

As we go through The Four Essential Questions together, I know that you too will discover that always-on-call is not a burden, but a source of constant pleasure, and the blessing of our lives.

WHAT IS OUR RESPONSIBILITY?

Always-on-call sounds frightening. When do we get time off? It feels as if the burden of responsibility would be overwhelming. Why not run, hide, lie, and wait?

I grew up with an intense feeling of responsibility, as I suspect most of us have. After all, it is what we were taught and trained, to be responsible, and of course we must be. But under what point of view?

If we take full responsibility, as if we are the cause and creator of all that is going on, then the burden is crushing. Who can survive under that? Well, some of us do for a while by "being strong." However, one day, that strength ebbs and we can't take it anymore. Many symptoms of this false responsibility are present in all of our lives. These symptoms range from physical sickness, to monetary distress, to unhealthy relationships.

"It's all my fault," is not a mantra we want to encourage no matter how many times we are told that it is. We may say it out of the desire to be humble and good, but ironically it makes us ego-driven, because we have given ourselves the power of Life itself.

"It's all my fault" also means "it's all my doing." Really—all of this is our doing? We, who cannot answer even the basic question of how the universe began, must accept responsibility for everything?

Yes and no. We are responsible, but not for what we have been trained to believe. We are responsible for thinking, choosing, and being aware of what is really going on. We are responsible for our perception, our point of view, and state of mind. We are responsible for our choice of perception. We are responsible for the act of shifting that perception.

Choosing and shifting perception changes the sense of the burden of responsibility. Responsibility then resides where it belongs, with that which is the only cause and creator, God. Our only responsibility is to be who we are intended to be. Our responsibility is to become aware of our running, hiding, lying, and waiting, and then to choose to let it go, and to live fully as our Unique Spiritual Blessing, our eternal spiritual identity.

We will go through The Four Essential Questions together, and together witness how they can relieve us of the false responsibility of cause and creator and return us to the true responsibility of choosing the correct perception and staying there.

Right Or Wrong

Do not condemn the judgment of another because it differs from your own. You may both be wrong. —Dandamis

As we ask ourselves these Four Essential Questions, it is important to know that the answer is neither right nor wrong. The intention of asking is to become aware. If we are running from a bear chasing us, then asking ourselves "Am I Running," is a good question to ask, and will make sure that we are moving.

If we are running from living our life, that's different. Then we must ask, "Why am I running, and what am I running from?"

If we are hiding from someone trying to hurt us, then the wisest answer to the question "Am I Hiding?" most likely will be, "yes!"

If we answer "yes" because we are hiding our light under a bushel so no one can receive the benefit of that light, then the answer gives us a new awareness of how we are living our life.

REACTING TO ILLUSIONS

Men who are devoid of the power of spiritual perception are unable to recognize anything that cannot be seen externally.—Paracelsus

Standing in the shower, I glanced up and saw what I thought were drops of water leaking from the top of the shower structure.

Since our days in our new home had been about "fix and repair" my first reaction was, "Oh no, not another thing to fix." Then I looked again and saw that what I was seeing was the reflection of the shower hooks on the ceiling. There was nothing to react about; the problem was an illusion.

Here's the thing that we often forget. All problems are an illusion. Uh huh, I know. We all know the many ways that problems do not feel like an illusion. However, just because they don't feel like an illusion, doesn't make them real.

This includes the often said, but usually misinterpreted, statement, "There are no accidents." It depends on how this statement is interpreted as to whether it is a True statement or not.

From a Spiritual Perception, this statement is correct because there are no accidents. They are an illusion, a misperception.

On the other hand, this statement is wrong when it is interpreted as something God would allow in order for good to result from the accident.

Of course, when what appears as an accident occurs, we have a choice of how to respond. When we remain in our highest understanding of God, Love, when confronted with the story, then that learning, that growth, that awareness, can, and often does, lead us to Good.

However, an illusion is an illusion, whether it is drops of water on the ceiling, or an accident, or mistreatment, hunger, lack, or sickness.

THEY ARE ALL ILLUSIONS.

In each case where an illusion tempts us to believe that it is real, we have a choice of reaction or replacement. We can react to the illusion or replace what the outside is telling us to be true, with what we know to be True.

Where does the statement that "anything that is not good is an illusion" come from? It comes from the Principle that God is Love, and Love is omnipresent and omniscience. This statement, this Principle, leaves absolutely no room for something other than Love as the only Reality.

The question is, "Doesn't Love give us these accidents and bad things in order to teach us?" The answer is, No! Omnipresent Love couldn't know anything other than Love.

It doesn't know us as humans needing to be taught a lesson. Divine Love isn't a glorified human personality.

It is a human interpretation of love that Love punishes, denies, or takes a break. Divine Love, as a Principle of being, knows nothing about anything other than Love Loving. This means that if we are not seeing direct evidence that Love is omnipresent, then we are being hypnotized by an illusion that Love is not omnipresent.

Feelings of fear, anger, hate, discouragement, despair, not knowing, lack, unhappiness, and doubt all stem from that illusion of the lack of omnipresent Love.

In the shower, I looked again at what appeared as something "bad" and saw my mistake. In life, we need to look again at the illusion representing itself as real, and see that right there is the evidence that it is an illusion.

It takes practice, but that is only because we have practiced so long in the illusion of lack that we have to rebuild our awareness of Truth. Within each of us is an already-present awareness that right where lack appears to be, is the direct experience of Love Loving Itself.

Either Love is omnipresent, or it isn't. Since what we determine and perceive as Reality is our personal reality, is what we experience, then whether we actually believe that Love is omnipresent, or have a direct experience that It is, or even if we don't believe it, why not go ahead and choose anyway the perception that It is.

WHY BOTHER?

41

Take your heart out into the vast fields of light and let it breathe. —Hafiz

What's the point anyway? Why bother to ask ourselves these questions? Why bother having more awareness?

There are esoteric answers, and practical answers. Here's an esoteric answer: Doing so helps dissolve misperceptions, including the main one, that we are separate from the divine Source. Here is a practical answer: Doing so increases our ability to live a happy and full life.

Both of these are certainly reasons for becoming more aware. However, the biggest reason will be that as we practice awareness, we will find ourselves. And not only that, we will find that we are wonderfully gifted, creative, resourceful, and loving.

Knowing that this is all about awareness, and then choosing what to do with that awareness, let's explore The Four Essential Questions, starting with the first one, "Am I Waiting?"

Make an agreement to yourself that no matter what you discover, you will not let the answer either dismay or excite you, but instead you will allow it to give you a strong basis upon which to make clear choices and set strong intents.

Are you ready? Let the exploration begin!

4

— · —

CHAPTER FOUR

*I*n our age the road to holiness necessarily passes through the world of action. —Dag Hammarskjold

Waiting is sometimes a good thing, and sometimes a bad thing. How do we know the difference? Once we have figured out the answer to that question, we will then need to know if what we are now ready to do is the right thing to do, or not. If we have all that straightened out, we will then need to know the right time to do it, because the right thing done at the wrong time makes it a wrong thing to do.

No wonder we have a habit of waiting!

If we use the example of reading this book, it is obvious that to read the book we have to begin, and the right thing to do is to read the book.

Obvious and easy, but still there are those of us who will put the book down at some point and then wait for a time, before we will pick it up again.

How long that will be depends on the reason why we put the book down in the first place.

It's apparent that there is more to waiting than meets the eye. To understand the mysteries of waiting, let's explore the subject further by asking ourselves these questions:

- How many ways do we wait?
- Who or what are we waiting for?
- Why wait at all?
- When is it the right choice to wait, and when it is it a stalling, or survival, tactic?
- How can we tell the difference?

STALLING

I had to laugh at myself while writing this section on waiting. I got to the paragraph above and "something" suggested I check my email. Once I did that, I then decided to answer people who had written. Then I "had" to clean out emails I didn't need any more. From there, I decided to take action on what some of the emails suggested I do. It was over an hour later before I realized I had stopped doing what I intended to do—write about waiting for at least one page—and had managed in the process to create a perfect symbol of the stalling form of waiting!

As I wrote those words, I realized I felt a little chilly, so I got up to put on a sweater, then I noticed that the phone was dusty so I went and got something to dust it with—stalling again. Why do we stall?

There are so many reasons for it you and I could probably spend a day listing them, so rather than figuring out the why of each one, let's come up with a way to minimize stalling, or perhaps to eliminate it all together.

Here it is, so simple we might think it useless, but it is a cornerstone of our actions. Become aware of it! Then treat it the same way we treat a distracted child. Gently, but with a clear focus, bring ourselves back to our stated intent.

Stated intent—what is that? We did a brief review of the idea of intent in the section of this book called *Right Thinking*. Let's pause now, (not stall), for a moment, and discuss the meaning and value of intent.

INTENT

The definition of intent revolves around purpose. This definition of intent—The state of a person's mind that directs his or her actions toward a specific object—is closely related to how we want to apply the concept of intent in our work together.

Intent is always present, but usually our intent is hidden from us, either because we are not aware of our unconscious choices or desires—which translate to intention—or because we have never learned how to consciously be aware of our intent.

I have often said, Whoever has the clearest intent wins, and this is absolutely true. By winning I mean, "leads the way." Since the way of those with a stronger intent may not be the way we thought we were going, or wanted to go, then all the more reason to be aware of, and to be present with, our own intent.

Intent is in every detail of life, so when we ignore it, we can lose our way in every situation in life—from what we buy at the store to how our life plays out. When we go to the store with the intent of only buying what is on our list, but end up buying the impulse item at the checkout counter, the store had the clearer intent.

When our intent is not to spend past our budget, but then we see something we want and put it on our credit card, then both the seller of the item, and the credit card company, had the clearer intent. At least one of them did not have our best interest at heart.

If we apply this idea to the more important parts of our life, it becomes obvious that it is always important to be aware of our intent.

Our intents are often formed by what we have been trained to believe is true, or right.

This means that it is important to be aware of the intent of those who are training us (schools, media, peer pressure, religious teachings, and political loyalties). Once we are aware of another's intent we can easily choose who, or what, we want to believe, because as we remember, what we perceive (believe) to be reality magnifies!

When our primary intent is to be what we really are, and to live our lives from the principles of good and happiness for all—beginning within our own lives—then we are less likely to be influenced by, or waylaid by, intentions that are false for us.

Using the advantage of the law that *perception rules*, we can stop trying so hard. We can stop powering our way through life. Instead, we can rest in our intention as we bring our state of mind and our point of view into harmony.

SQUIRREL INTENTION

One animal that truly represents clear intent, and intention, is the squirrel. Anyone who has ever put up a bird feeder knows that eventually it will be necessary to outwit the squirrels. We have watched squirrels study a bird feeder, and know that it is only a matter of time before its intention, and its skill in carrying out its intention, will win over our intention to stop it.

The squirrel doesn't feel guilty for having such a strong intent. It is not focusing on winning anything; it does not carry any personal grudges, or feel competition with anyone else, including us humans. It is not out to hurt anyone. No, it simply has a clear idea of what it is, and what it wants to accomplish.

If I could get inside of a squirrel's thought, I am sure I would find that it also never doubts that somewhere, somehow, there is a way, and it will figure it out. A squirrel doesn't stop trying because it falls off the feeder, or makes a fool of itself. A squirrel demonstrates patient intention.

I watched a butterfly trying to get out from under the canopy on our deck. It fluttered and flew everywhere. I tried to direct it to fly down to get out, but it was much too busy trying too hard. It had a strong intention to get out, but it was not a patient, and wise, intention.

If the butterfly could have borrowed a page from the squirrel, it would have paused, and watched. It would have looked around and discovered the many avenues of escape. It would have known that it got in, so there must be a way out. I watched it for over an hour and it still had not escaped.

Sometimes it was just a quarter of an inch away from edge of the canopy. A short pause there, feeling the breeze, listening to direction, would have released it in that moment.

This kind of frantic intention that the butterfly demonstrated, is not based on wisdom, but on fear. We want to set our intentions just like the squirrel's; patient, wise, confident, and skilled. Since we have the ability to do so, we will also add the extra quality of looking at the big picture. We can ask ourselves the question, "Will this be good for all for now, and into the future?"

First Intent

There is a theme running through the show, *Battlestar Galatica*, that relates to this idea of first intent. The idea is that once you find, and accept, your role in life, the ego drops away and life really begins. Or, said differently, once we recognize that our first intent is to be the intent of the Divine, because we are Its idea in action, then we begin to discover the unique expression of our life.

There is a segment of the TV show *So You Think You Can Dance*, where dancers who are in the "bottom" perform a quick solo that is designed to show exactly who they are, and what they bring to dance. It's called, "dancing for your life."

They are encouraged to bring all of themselves to that dance, reveal their heart, share their passion, and be entirely present in those moments, so that all that they are is visible to others.

When they are willing to set that as their intent, and they fully sink into that intent, their solos are beyond description. And the audience can tell when they don't.

If we can tell the quality of intent of a performance on stage, in an area most of us are not trained to observe, imagine how easy it is to tell when people are not "dancing for their life" in their lives.

We, of course, know when we are not. In the dance world, this is called "marking." Just marking the moments, standing where you are supposed to be, giving a rough estimate of how it goes, using as little energy as possible, this is marking. Most of us live our lives this way, just marking it, marking time, using up time, so that we don't have to "bring it on."

I could put this section on intent under every question, but I think it fits best under waiting. At least in the dance world we could claim to be saving our energy for an upcoming performance. However, what performance are we waiting for in our life?

It doesn't work anyway. Marking a dance doesn't build the strength, or commitment to the movement, that is needed for a brilliant performance. Marking life, waiting for a performance that isn't even scheduled, is tragic. We have been designed to bring the unique blessing that we are into every moment. Make that your first intent, and see how fast the false habit of waiting for what is already present melts away.

In the TV show *Lie To Me*, there is a young woman who demonstrates a natural talent for the work. In one scene, she complains that she is not getting enough recognition, while at the same time she is doubting her ability. Her boss says to her, "You still don't get it yet, do you? You have a talent. And guess what. It's not about you. It's not about me. And the talent, and what you do, are not just for you anymore."

This is true for each of us.

We each have a talent, and it is never about us. It is what we are designed to do. Instead of intellectually talking about ideas and doing nothing, it is time to take action. This willingness to be who we truly are, to live as we have been designed to live, as the action of the Divine, and to take our place in the world is our first intent.

It's Just Too Much

"It's just too much, I am overwhelmed and under appreciated. No matter what I do, it doesn't give me any satisfaction, and it is never good enough." Do you ever think, or say, something like this?

In today's rush-rush-rush world with its speeded up technology, and information overload, combined with the appearance of lack in so many lives, "It's just too much" is a common feeling among us all.

Sometimes it is hard to remember the reason why we do anything. Our society focuses on the rich, famous, and the beautiful—or how to get there—and rarely is the contentment to lead a simple, loving, and fulfilling life, celebrated.

Here, in the midst of this false sense of what life is about, we must find our own awareness of what happiness is for us, and learn how to live that elegant, and contented, life. This means that we have to step out of the worldview of what we thought we are supposed to do, and by listening within, find the path we are meant to walk, and then get up, and live our life fully.

There is always much to do; that is what life is about. Can you imagine if the force we call Life, would suddenly appear depressed and overwhelmed? Plopping Itself down in front of the TV, It would declare, "It is just too much, I can't do this anymore." Of course, this would never happen! Life is always about being Life and Love. It is not waiting for someone to notice It, (we rarely do), or appreciate It, or enjoy It. It just does what It does.

The joy is in being fully what we are, and living the simple beauty of life by letting go of what we no longer need. The trick lies in revealing to ourselves who we are, and that is exactly what we are doing together as we ask ourselves The Four Essential Questions, and then listen honestly, and without judgment, to the answers.

LIFE JAMS

Have you ever been in a traffic jam? Once traveling from Connecticut to Ohio, Del and I were in three of them. Two of them lasted long enough that we turned off the car and waited for an hour or more before being able to move on. In all of them, we never saw the cause even though the result was over

10 miles of stopped traffic. However, once the cause of the jam was removed, the traffic flowed as if it had never happened.

Did you ever sit by a little stream of water after a rain, and put sticks in it to watch the water back up? Of course, we have all seen big streams of water backed up as one log, or other obstacle, gets stuck and backs up more debris until the stream stops running, and begins to flood.

Life jams work the same way. One thing gets stuck in our mind, and a life jam begins. It can feel like nothing is moving in our life, or it can be an overwhelming flood of feeling that it's just "too much."

We react to this life jam in many ways. We can feel angry, depressed, tired, manic, confused, or even live in a state of "who cares." Since life jams are not visual, like a traffic jam or a blocked stream, we often don't understand what has stopped the flow. We just know that our life is not working.

The good news about all jams is that all it takes is the removal of the first obstacle for the traffic, stream, and our life to begin to flow again. But, how do we find the cause of our life jam? Often we already know the cause, but haven't believed it could be so simple; or the problem could feel too hard to let it go.

Years ago, I was in a life jam. Nothing I did worked. Nothing happened. I worked hard, tried hard, used all the ideas I could think of that always worked before, but they didn't work this time. However, all along I was hearing an inner voice telling me that I wanted to paint.

Nevertheless, since nothing was working in my life, I had "reasons" why I couldn't paint. No money, and no time, were two of them. I felt that I had to get out of the jam I was living in first. Finally, out of ideas, I decided to listen to the inner voice again. It said, "Paint." I said "No money, no time." It said, "Paint."

I thought that meant I would have to buy an easel, paints, and brushes. Eventually it occurred to me that I could afford a can of wall paint, and a brush, so that's what I did.

Within days of my beginning to paint my walls, my life started to flow again. In this case, my life jam began by my wanting things to go my way and by not honoring an inner desire that I had because I felt that I didn't deserve it. I was listening to a belief, a committed thought pattern, not to my intuition.

Life jams are also caused by not wanting to, or not knowing how to, do something. Or having too many things to do without knowing what to do first.

The answer is again: listen. Perhaps the thing we feel we have to do doesn't really need to be done, or can be done a different way. Ask for help for the thing you don't know how to do.

Take one thing—anything—and lift it out of the jam either by doing it, or by getting rid of it. Your life jam will loosen by doing one thing at a time, just as a tangled knot in a necklace unfolds by taking out one knot at a time.

Sometimes it takes someone outside of ourselves to see the cause of our life jam.

Often in speaking to clients, I hear them state the cause, but they still can't see it themselves. If I can guide them in a way that opens their eyes to their thought pattern, they can easily release that thought, and the actions, or the non-actions, that follow from it, and let life flow again.

Spirit always flows.

It's our thoughts, and the perception that follows them, that cause life jams. Our belief systems, past and present, are as solid as matter. In fact, what appears as our life and matter is our firm commitment to what we believe to be true. Unless it is based on big R Reality, it is always a misperception of what is actually happening.

Matching Reasons To Actions

You miss 100% of the shots you never take.—Wayne Gretsky

Sometimes we wait because we can't figure out why to take an action. Sometimes waiting is a good thing; we call this kind of waiting "pausing." Other times there is a direct need to take action now, but we can't get ourselves to move, and that kind of waiting is what we want to eliminate. One way to stop waiting, and start doing, is to find enough reasons to take action that mean something to you. This takes some self-observation, but that is exactly what you are doing as you ask The Four Essential Questions and observe the answers.

Here's what I learned when observing myself while looking for how to match reasons and actions. First, I realized I need a curtain-opening scenario in order to get myself motivated.

When I was taking ballet as a teenager, I got bored with it, until my teacher announced a recital. Suddenly, for me, there was a reason to go on, and all thoughts of quitting vanished. In fact, I remember that performance like a gem in a crown of my life.

As part of the promotion, the producers of the program had a picture of me taken because I was the Sugar Plum Fairy.

The photographer said to me, "You will remember this time and this picture for the rest of your life." That proved to be very true. Although for the next 16 years I was part of many performances, and loved them all, that one has stood out to me. The picture taken that day hangs on my parents' bedroom wall, and my children, and now my grandchildren, have asked me about that time.

What's important about this is that I discovered a reason that motivates me. However, since performing is something I no longer desire to do, it may appear I can no longer use that as a reason and motivation. The opposite is true

To bring that reason up to date, instead of focusing on the outside picture called "performing," I looked at the essence of what was happening at that moment, and realized there was something more than just the performance that I loved. In fact, I loved it even more: It was the community of performers. It was the anticipation of something marvelous, and slightly scary, that we prepared for together, and that together we would experience. When I design something, and I am thinking of doing it around these same ideas and principles, I am on the road to doing what I want to do, instead of stalling or waiting.

Another key element in doing a performance is the idea of a curtain going up. Standing backstage, we would peak out at the audience, and feel the tingles of anticipation knowing that there were people out there waiting for us to appear.

We hoped that we were prepared. Of course, we had to be, because the curtain was going up! It didn't matter if we were the performers, or the technical crew running the show, we all had to be ready, no excuses, because the show had to go on.

Applying this idea to the life I lead today, I noticed that there was a correlation between the feelings of too much to do that seem like a task, and not a joy, and therefore causing inertia in me, and not having a curtain going up type of deadline.

So I began to set deadlines that I knew would stretch me, but I also knew I could meet. To make it a curtain going up deadline I needed an audience on the other end, so I set up expectations. I let people know when to expect things from me.

These expectations range from when I reply to emails, to what day the new website will be unveiled, or to what day people will be coming to the house for a party.

When I am really stuck in the waiting mode, I use another way to motivate myself; it may sound morbid, but in reality, it is based on love. I ask myself, "What if you died today; how would you feel if this weren't done?" This is useful for tiny things, like leaving the house picked up when I walk out the door, and larger things, like writing this book, or putting my papers in order.

I have found other reasons that I can use to move myself to take action.

I have discovered that if I feel that what I am doing will change lives, I am motivated to take action. To get into this mode, I often ask myself, "Does someone need for me to do this? Is someone waiting for someone like me to make that phone call, write that book, or go to the store and pick up groceries?" If the answer is "yes," I am much more likely to take action.

Designing a system is another motivation for me. And if it is a system, or tool, that I can leave behind for another to use to improve their day-to-day life, then the excitement of this idea impels me to action. If I combine these ingredients—the community, the rise-of-the-curtain deadline, how would I feel if I didn't do it, is someone waiting for me to do this, and a system that will make a difference—then I am highly motivated.

Another trick I use is this: I never ask myself this question when I am in a stalling or waiting mode: "Do you want to?" This may sound opposite to what I am talking about, but it is exactly the same thing. The reason I don't ask that question, is the answer will always be "no." "No I don't want to get up, no I don't want to exercise this morning, no I don't want to write today, no I don't want to call anyone, no I don't want to do my work, no and no and no!"

Instead, I give myself reasons that inspire me to get up, exercise, write, call, and work. The person we ask, "Do you want to," when we are in the waiting-stalling mode is not really who we are.

In fact, it is the counterfeit of ourselves, whose intention is to stop us from fully living our lives.

Just as we do not give credence to children throwing a temper tantrum, or listen to people whom we know mean to do us harm, we do not listen to that voice that is not us, because it does not have our best interest at heart, and it is always lying.

You can read more about this voice in this book under the heading What Voice Is Yours?

Now it is your turn to listen within, and observe your life, to find what reasons motivate you to take action. Find inspiring ideas, and they will help lead you out of the quicksand of waiting.

WAITING FOR OTHERS

I never teach my pupils. I only attempt to provide the conditions in which they can learn. —Albert Einstein

How many times have we all waited for someone before going on with a part of our lives? Pardon me if you are a man, but speaking to the women reading this—how many times have you waited for a man? I suppose it's our training. After all, there was a time when all we were supposed to do was find a man, settle down, and let him take care of our many children, and us, for forever after.

Oh wait, was it so long ago, or are we still on that page? Witness shows like *The Bachelor*.

We are not that woman anymore, are we? On the other hand, perhaps we are, just not so obviously. I am not advocating that we do not choose to please each other, but many of us make choices based on the counterfeit *what if* factor. Instead of the *what if* of imagination and allowing our ideas to flow, it is the *what if* I do this, will it win his, or her, love and respect? Or the *what if* I do this and I lose him or her?

Then there is the I can't factor. How many times have we all said 'I can't, until I have someone to help me?"

We often make standing still choices based on the what if and I can't beliefs. We sacrifice our time and our desires while waiting for the "perfect someone." Sometimes we think that someone is already in our lives, but that person is choosing to live a different way, while we wait, or table our desires, so that person can be fulfilled.

In one of my long-ago relationships, after noticing that once again my waiting for him did not stop him from living his life the way he wanted to, without a glance at what I might desire, I said to myself, "Beca, it is time to get a life." It took the breaking of many old habits, and sticking with the first intent, but today, I do have a life—my life.

Say this to yourself, "It is time to get a life!" No more waiting for a person, place, or thing. Take the step forward that moves you into the life that is waiting for you. It is in that life, and only in that life, that those that you wish were present now can find you.

GIFTING YOUR FUTURE SELF

Instead of giving our future self a problem, wouldn't it be more fun to give our future self a gift? Future self, as in who we will be tomorrow, later today, next year, or ten years from now. We all do gift our future self sometimes.

We make enough in one meal to have it later. We save some money to spend it later. We mow the grass during the week so that we can go away on the weekend.

However, more often, we give our future self a problem instead of a gift. We spend more money than we have, we don't clean up our mess, we cover up problems, we don't take good care of ourselves, we don't learn new skills to keep up, we don't read the instructions on something we are putting together, we don't listen when someone is telling us something.

Oh yes, this list could go on and on.

Instead of making resolutions about what we are going to do, which for the most part is giving our future self a chance to feel guilty because we don't do it, why not switch it up and think instead, "How can I give my future self a gift?" Of course, we will be asking our future self to pass it on to its future self. These gifts are not designed to make our future self into something less, but to enable it to be more.

Since not gifting our future self is often our habit, I developed a few ways for breaking that habit. For example, I notice that I often give my future self a problem because I put things off until there is enough pressure to get it done, either external or internal. Noticing that, I use the methods described in the section of this book called Matching Reasons To Actions to help me break the habit of waiting, and instead put it back under my own choice of when and how.

"Have a place," is an example of another method I use for making sure I am thinking of my future self. Packing for trips is a good example of how this works. As I think what I need for a trip, long before I go on it, I drop what I need into a bag that sits on top of my suitcase. A few days before the trip I open the suitcase, and the bag, and as I go about my days I willy-nilly toss into it whatever occurs to me that I will need on the trip. The day I actually pack, most of what I need is already there.

There are many more ways to provide for our future self. The interesting outcome is that as we gift our future self, we find that we are gifting our current self too. We live more in the moment, not the past. We find ourselves less stressed and more excited about life.

How does this all fit into Spiritual Perception, which is of course always the theme?

Here it is: Love providing for Its future "Self" is the Principle of big R Reality. It's not how our five senses report it to be, but how we **know** It to be, using both logic and internal awareness. God—I know I am temporarily making God "human like"—lives as the moment of "curtain going up" and "having a place." God has to have every star in its right place, bird feathers attached, insect feelers operational, flower buds prepared, tree roots anchored, and every hair on our head numbered at all times.

As we gift our future self with small and large acts of kindness, it is a constant reminder that we are the recipients of Love gifting Itself in all Its unique forms and ways. Not because it has to, but because that is how it works. Knowing this, and living from it, is the best gift we can give our future selves. As an outcome of this gift to ourselves, we give to everyone our lives touch. Gift your future self by living in your present self, and pass it on.

WHAT ARE WE WAITING FOR?

I thought it would be interesting to put some of the things people wait for in the form of a list. Why not put a check mark beside the ones that mean something to you? Then notice which one happens today. Noticing gives us power to make conscious choices.

For example, the first word on this list is clarity.

It might seem as if we want to wait for clarity. However, waiting for clarity just might take a lifetime. Why not pause for direction, take a step forward, and pause again for more awareness and focus. Pause, and listen, for the still small voice for what action to take—take the action—and pause again. We call this POL (Pause, Observe, Listen). Then act, and do it again.

Here's A List: What Are We Waiting For?

- Clarity
- Focus
- Enough reasons
- To know what to do
- For the time to be right
- For the right age
- For enough: money, time, knowledge, etc.
- To be out of debt
- Until we can do the whole thing at once
- Until we can do it perfectly
- A partner
- A team
- Friends and family to agree with us

- Until we live someplace else
- Funding

Why not add to this list? Then when you ask yourself, "Am I Waiting" you will have a "cheat-sheet" to help you uncover what you are waiting for. This awareness is the beginning of freedom. Here is an example of waiting, written by a member of The Shift® Community, Diana Cormier:

"While reflecting, the thought of waiting came to mind. If I look back on my life, it seems if I were to attach just one word to summarize my life that word would be waiting. Waiting for life to start, waiting for love, waiting for the right job, waiting to graduate from school, waiting for a vacation, waiting for happiness to start, waiting for, waiting for, waiting for. A definition of the word wait from Webster's is to remain inactive or in a state of repose, as until something expected happens (often followed by for, till, or until): to wait for the bus to arrive. (Repose = absence of movement.)

"If we find ourselves in a constant state of waiting, aren't we implying that good is only something in the future? Or perhaps we are looking back at a good time in our lives and then we are believing that good is only in the past. To be in a constant state of waiting, and therefore implying that good is ours only in the future, and only if a certain chain of events takes place in a certain way, is limiting our experience now. Mostly because this constant "wait state," in nature, never becomes the future. To wait for good means that we are deprived of good now. To be deprived of good now means that we believe it is possible to be deprived of God's expression now, and that we are an expression of Divine Love only in the future, but not now.

"We never have to do something, or wait for something, to be Love's expression. God's reflection is now and always. God isn't waiting for something before expressing Itself. Divine Love is always expressed, and that expression is us. We are now and always the manifestation of God's perfect Infinite expression, full of nothing but perfection and good.

"I don't need anything or anyone to rescue me from another person. That other person is an individual expression of Divine Love as much as I am. Love is reflected in love.

"I am not governed or controlled, either energetically or mentally, by another person. My energy and my well-being is protected and governed by Divine Love. Two ideas of Love—two people—can do nothing but support, enhance, and bless each other.

"What blesses one, blesses all. I am free of any dependence. My happiness, love, energy, and experience is dependent on God alone, not on any other person. I don't have to wait for inspiration in order to heal; I am the inspired expression of God. My thoughts are God's thoughts; God's thoughts are the only thoughts I can have."

Thank you, Diana, for this example of moving on from false waiting!

OK, now for the rest of us, what are we waiting for? Start now! Don't wait to learn the next three questions, or until you finish the book, or after you take a shower, or until the first of the month, or until you have someone to do this exercise with you, or until you know everything. Start now. Ask yourself, "Am I Waiting?"

5

CHAPTER FIVE

Yesterday we obeyed kings and bent our necks before emperors. But today we kneel only to truth, follow only beauty, and obey only love. —Khalil Gibran

As we discussed earlier, there are no right and wrong answers to these questions. The questions are designed to do two things; help us become aware of what we are thinking and doing, and to assist us in making clear, conscious choices.

Of course, there are times we may choose to run because that is the wisest thing to do at the time. To get out of an abusive marriage, I chose to run. However, eventually I had to stop running, go back, and collect what I could of what I had to leave behind when I ran. Perhaps if I hadn't been hiding from the truth of what was happening for so long it may never have escalated to running, and instead I could have dealt with it in a way that was less difficult for everyone involved.

If I had asked myself *The Four Essential Questions* way back then it absolutely would have changed the lives of many people. Now, instead of running from the memory, I choose consciously to forgive myself and everyone involved; we were all blinded at one time or another by our misperceptions.

Let's look at some of the ways that we run.

RUNNING FROM THE PAST

There are obvious ways that we run, hide, and lie about the past; like moving away and rarely or never going back home because we don't want to face what we have run from. Let's look at some of the less obvious ways we run, and how we can choose to stop running, replacing the issue instead with something we can live with.

Here's an example: I spent many years working as a Certified Financial Planner. For a few of those years, one of my clients was a large municipality that allowed everyone who had a 401k to trade their own account. This meant that my phone rang all day long. On the other end of the phone were people I barely knew, and who were not following any of the ideas that my "real" clients would follow, such as patience, wisdom, and holding on to what was good.

These people were day trading, and for the most part did not know what they were doing.

I hated that phone ringing because I knew I would be talking to people who wanted something quickly, and that wanting would more often than not lead them to losing their money, because they were not interested in listening to my advice. Now, many years later, I still don't like the phone ringing very much.

You could say that because I have set my life up so that phone rarely rings, that I am running from the phone. That would be true except for one tiny difference. Instead of running, I consciously set up my life this way. I am willing to let the phone ring while at the same time providing ways to talk to people in other ways. This means that when the phone does ring, it is for all the right reasons.

When we say that we can't do something because it reminds us of the past, we are running.

The problem with running away from something in the past is that it keeps us from seeing what is present now. A state of mind of disgust, or fear, or any similar emotion, blinds us to what is right in front of us.

When we face a task filled with resentment, or sorrow, or anger, or simply the statement, "I won't do it," we are running, and most likely running from a memory of the past. There are two interesting things about memories—one, they are always wrong, and two, (which supports number one) they can always be changed.

I have a vivid memory of a time when I lived in Venice, CA. In this memory, I would walk out my back door, walk up the bank at the side of the house, and go paint pictures at a friend's home. It's a lovely memory. For years, I saw this vision in my head, when I recalled that time.

However, one day I realized this was a merged memory, because I never left by the back door, and there was no bank on the side of our house in Venice.

Although I did paint with a friend when we lived in Venice, the memory of the bank on the side of the house existed from the home we lived in when I was a teenager. I actually can't picture where my friend's home really was in Venice anymore; it has been replaced with a false memory.

Our memories of the past are a mixed bag of some things that happened, some things that didn't happen that way, how we were feeling about it then, and how we feel about it now. Talk to someone else about that time, and they will have a different memory of that time than you do.

Therefore, we can now choose to have different feelings about any event in the past. Why is this important? Remember that perception is what determines our reality, and if we really want to live abundantly in every area of our life, it's time to reframe our past perception, and choose one that more closely matches what we know and desire now.

Perhaps you are not interested in living abundantly. Maybe you like the excuses why you can't do something. Okay, then keep running from what never happened. Eventually you will have to do this shift work anyway, so since you are thinking about it now, why not now?

Not Looking

Have you ever not opened your snail mail, not read your email, not answered the phone, or not opened a package? What a great running technique. It's a funny one though, because when we do the "not looking" behavior, most of us are clueless why we are doing it.

What do we think? That if we don't open the email, it doesn't exist? As much as we may try to tell ourselves that it doesn't exist until we look at it, (like Schrödinger's cat) the truth is, as we well know, that it does. Therefore, it weighs on us. In the back of our mind, we know there is much unfinished business. People have written us and they expect a response from us.

Each time we run, and don't look, the urge to run and not look gets bigger because of the built-up pressure of not doing what we know we "should" or want to do.

Here are some steps to use to stop this particular running habit. First, become aware of this behavior. Next, pay attention to what you think will happen if you look.

Will something more be expected of you than you think you can handle? Is it just one more thing on a very full plate? Do you think you won't know how to answer? Are you punishing the person for something? Are you afraid of that person? Do you think you will say the wrong thing?

Don't judge the answers, just notice how you feel. Accept that it is okay to feel that way. However, recognize that the not looking isn't solving anything, and then put into practice a step-by-step approach that works for you.

One Step At A Time

Sometimes we run because there is just too much to do, or we don't know what to do next.

Here's a way to stop that practice—one-step-at-a-time. We have all heard of this concept before.

We know what it means, see the big picture, but don't be overwhelmed by it. Instead, take one-step-at-a-time and you will arrive at your destination.

It's an easy to apply tool to add to our perception shifting basket, and one that makes life so much easier if we utilize it.

It is easier to take one step at a time running up a hill than it is to look up and notice how much further there is to go. One-step-at- time, one foot in front of another, and the top of the hill arrives almost without noticing it.

I saw evidence of how powerful this concept is even if you are as light as a bird, because it was bird feet that demonstrated it to me.

We have a railing that goes around our deck, and after a snowstorm the snow on the railing was over 12 inches high. One section of the railing is a landing area for the birds as they fly to the feeder hanging under the roof of our porch. These are little birds that barely make a mark in the snow when they touch down.

The next day, after the snowstorm, the snow on the railing was still over 12 inches high except for one section. The section where the birds land was packed down to only a few inches. It was bird feet that did this, one tiny foot at a time, one little light step at a time.

Within each of our hearts, there is a calling to do something.

Too often, we are overwhelmed with the idea of it and stop listening, walling it off, hoping that it will disappear, and then we start running. This never works, does it? Because the desire and calling never disappear. Like the water behind the dike in the Little Dutch Boy Tale, there will always be a leak, and it will flood out into our lives.

Or we will stand there with our finger in the hole in the dike, not being able to do anything else.

Instead of running, we could take a cue from the birds. The reason the birds land on the railing is to get to the food. In a very real sense these birds have a calling to find food. The calling we are hearing within our hearts is the same thing. It is our food, hanging there, safe under the roof, ready to feed us forever.

We don't have to know how to do all the details of what is calling us. We don't have to understand where it will lead. We don't have to qualify; we don't have to earn it. We just have to be willing to put one foot in front of the other and accept it for what it is—the essence of what we call God—calling us to bloom as our Unique Spiritual Blessing.

This calling carries with it all that it needs to support and sustain it. We can trust in this Truth. Instead of fighting who we are, we can love it. Not love the small personality, or ego that we think we are, but instead we can love the God qualities that we represent. We can enjoy them, and we can share them. If we don't love them, we can't say we love God, can we?

Loving ourselves is not an ego trip. It is a step into humility when we recognize the Truth of ourselves. In this state of humility and Love, we can get out of our own way and step forward into what is calling us, because it is simply our awareness of God becoming present as our lives.

We can take those little steps, no matter how small, no matter how light, because each step does make a difference. All that is required of us is to be the active awareness of Good. And in Truth, what could be easier than that? One-step-at-a-time, it's that simple.

Learning Something New

An Age is called dark not because the light fails to shine, but because people refuse to see it.—James Albert Michener

We often run from the idea of learning something new. I should actually say that adults run from the idea of learning something new. Children are in the constant business of learning something new—exploring, discovering, and open to adventure.

I often hear adults say "I don't want to grow up," and in the same breath they say, "I don't want to learn that new thing, or new idea." Well then, act like a child and learn new things! Better yet, retain that childlikeness while choosing to grow up, because growing up is a glorious event. As a grown up we have the means and wisdom to constantly learn new things, and in doing so we will open up to ideas and worlds that were hidden to us when we chose to run from the new.

Yes, I know that in the information-overload era that we live in, everything can feel like a learning curve we can't meet, and the more we feel we have to learn just to keep up, the more we are tempted to run from learning.

In my writing and consulting business I always have new software programs to learn, and upgraded computers to purchase. Each time I have a choice—either run from the learning, stall as long as possible, or put aside time to learn, grateful to see so many symbols of the Infinite Intelligence of the divine Mind. This is the same choice that we all have. We are the representation of Infinite Intelligence, and therefore already contain all that we need to know to live our life productively.

FROM WHO YOU ARE

Our deepest fear is not that we are inadequate. Our deepest fear is that we are powerful beyond measure. It is our light, not our darkness that frightens us.
We ask ourselves, who am I to be brilliant, gorgeous, talented, and fabulous? Actually, who are we not to be? You are a child of God.
Your playing small doesn't serve the world. There's nothing enlightened about shrinking so that other people won't feel insecure around you.
We were born to make manifest the glory of God that is within us. It's not just in some of us, it's in everyone. And as we let our own light shine, we unconsciously give other people permission to do the same.
As we are liberated from our own fears, our presence automatically liberates others.—Maryann Williamson

This famous poem by Marianne Williamson says it all. We all, at one time or another, have run from our light. Some of us have kept on running.

BECA LEWIS

The other side of this equation happens when we are dealing with a relationship issue with someone.

If we hold the Truth in our thinking about the person we have the issue with, and treat that person as if they are a child of God (not angry, spiteful, depressed, incapable, etc.) then one of two things will happen. Either the person will move closer to us because of a willingness to live as the child of God, or that person will move away from us.

Sometimes we are that person, running from the Truth of ourselves.

We may run to the easier path, to those that will treat us as we are used to being treated—because it feels familiar to be treated as if we are a victim, or angry, or depressed, or incapable. On the other hand, we may simply run away from everyone, just in case someone might see the lie that we are living.

You know that saying, "You can run, but you can't hide." This is certainly a true statement, which makes it a perfect lead-in to the next question.

6

— · —

CHAPTER SIX

*L*et yourself be silently drawn by the stronger pull of what you really are. —Rumi

Many of us refuse to reveal ourselves to anyone. Perhaps we feel this is an invasion of privacy. This makes complete sense. We do need to keep things private that need to be private. On the other hand, we live in a world where one fast Google search will reveal massive amounts of information about us. This kind of visibility isn't going to go away.

The question is, how are we choosing to be visible? Of course, it is wise and prudent to hide from view many personal and financial details. We can monitor what is being said about us, and do our best to make sure that what is being said is accurate.

However, many of us hide from those who would benefit us if we would just let them into our lives.

Hiding behind a wall from those who would help us, not only does not serve us, but it also doesn't really work. We live in a world of constant visibility, and yet we hide the most important part of ourselves, our essential expression, our Unique Spiritual Blessing, from everyone—beginning with ourselves. When we ask and honestly answer the question, "Am I Hiding" we can make conscious choices, rather than hiding "just because."

ISOLATION

Call it a clan, call it a network, call it a tribe, call it a family. Whatever you call it, whoever you are, you need one.—Jane Howard

When I am struggling with something, I have to force myself to not withdraw and hide. Hiding when we are troubled, and isolating ourselves away from those that could, and would, help us is a dangerous choice. This type of isolation is the perfect breeding ground for the dark, and unlikable thoughts, that got us there in the first place.

A friend called this false isolation. As I thought about that idea, the image of a pack of animals running away from a lion entered my mind. As I mentally watched, I saw how the lion separated one animal from the pack and then easily tired it out, hunted it down, and killed it.

This sounds rather gruesome, but in many ways, it is an accurate picture.

When we are struggling, we need protection and support, not isolation.

The solution is to join a pack. Get yourself a circle of angels. It's amazing how many of us call ourselves a loner. I certainly have. Yet we are never alone anyway. We are all part of the whole.

I watched a documentary about how DNA works. The commentator described the division between those that believe we have evolved and those that believe that God created us all in seven days.

I visually, and emotionally, stepped back from that division and listened instead to the symbol of DNA. Instead of seeing it as a divisor, I saw it as a symbol that proves both theories, when we begin with the premise that we are all One.

To make this overly simple doesn't negate the idea, so here goes. We all have the same DNA. There are two factors that make us different, the ordering of the particles, and the timing of switches. For example, we all have the possibilities of patterning. It is the arrangement of particles and the timing of switches that determines if we will have the spots of a leopard, the coloring of a fish, or freckles.

Starting with the correct premise that God is the intelligent creator, and all that we see is the outcome of Its creation, do you see the magnificent symbol of DNA, and the oneness of both ideas?

Understanding DNA as the symbol of the intelligent creator and abundance of living creatures as the outcome, evolution becomes just a variety of ways that the One Painter has painted Its ideas.

Let's go back to the idea of finding ourselves a circle of angels. To do this, find a group of people that see and value you for who you are—not for how you act, for what you have, or for what you say—but for the essence of yourself.

Find a group of people that want you to bloom in your life without any personal prejudice of what that will look like. Find a group of people who are willing to take action.

Band together in a pack and connect with them. Get organized in a way that works for all of you. Stay together. Protect each other. Honor and respect each other. Always be present for them, as they will be for you.

When we are tempted to isolate ourselves in times of trouble, let's remember the picture of the weaker animal that is easily hunted down by a predator. Then picture an elephant tribe that circles around a member of their group that is in trouble, and protects it from danger until it is strong again. Join a pack, join a circle of angels, and protect and be protected.

It is true, United we stand, divided we fall.—Aesop

Silly Reasons

One of the happiest times of my life almost never happened because I didn't like the idea of going out at night, and I didn't want to miss a rerun of my favorite show at the time, Perry Mason.

Go ahead, laugh, but seriously, those were my reasons. I had to force myself past these two issues to do something I knew would take up every extra minute of my life, which I didn't feel I had many of, for the next few years.

But I did it. I started a dance company while attending college full time, raising children, and working at least one part-time job to support my family.

I had many excuses that were even better than not wanting to go out at night, and missing Perry Mason, but my human sense of myself tried to stop me from experiencing full happiness with something that silly. I could have used any of the other reasons, and anybody would have understood, and agreed with me, that I was too busy, but when I listened within, I found those two excuses were the real reasons I was stopping myself.

Once those hidden reasons were revealed, I had a choice of accepting them as real, or setting them aside and doing it anyway, which is what I did.

The result of choosing what looked so hard to do was a time that everyone involved still recalls as a brilliantly happy experience, full of priceless memories.

I heard a woman explain why she was not fully expressing herself by saying, "I guess I am delaying my happiness." Don't we all delay our happiness at least some of the time?

Why we do this isn't important. We could take lots of time and drill down into our human situation and find perfectly acceptable reasons for delaying or never accepting happiness, with and as, our life.

However, why waste time with the why we aren't happy, when knowing why we are not happy is not necessary to be happy.

In fact, this is often another excuse for delaying happiness. Instead, let's move to happiness now by stepping out of the human why and why not. Let's go to where happiness is a quality that always exists, and can never, ever, be replaced by sorrow.

Where is that? Not in the human duality point of view. Not within the state of mind of not being good enough, or it not being the right time, or in feeling guilty, feeling superior, feeling old, or feeling useless.

It is not found in the thought that we are the wrong sex, wrong height, wrong weight, or lacking intelligence or skill—no—nor it is found anywhere within the human duality point of view.

The *where* is here and the time is now. It is within the understanding that what we call the force of life, the substance of being, is Mind Itself, the Infinite intelligence of Love, Loving Itself. Here is where happiness is the substance of our being. Not something that must be attained, but what is, now.

There is no need to plead that the love of God shall fill our hearts as though He were unwilling to fill us...Love is pressing around us on all sides like air. Cease to resist and instantly love takes possession.—Amy Carmichael

We can see it everywhere, a baby's laugh, a bird song, a tree in the breeze, a flower blooming. These are the symbols, the signs, the proof of Love as the only cause and creator.

We will see more of these outward expressions only as we begin within the Truth of being and stay there.

What appears without will become closer and closer to the essence of Truth, not because we are creating it or making it happen, but because we are lifting the veil from our eyes, or more accurately our perception. The mist dissolves, revealing Life Living Itself.

Happiness cannot be stopped from being the essence of our lives by those seemingly logical reasons that the dualist worldview gives when we see those claims for what they are—lies.

We can never change an outward appearance by remaining unhappy, but when we choose an inward happiness, it will shift what appears without in ways far beyond any human outlining.

We can choose to be happy now, even when we are surrounded by people who are not happy, and who have good reasons why they aren't. If we really want to help them, we must step out of that story and light the way for them by revealing happiness, in and as, our life now.

It doesn't need to take years, months, days, or even hours to be happy now. When we stand in Truth, the Truth will set us free.

I am still determined to be cheerful and happy in whatever situation I may be, for I have also learned from experience that the greater part of our happiness or misery depends upon our dispositions, and not upon our circumstances.—Martha Washington

HIDING IN THE NOISE

Many of us hide in the noise. You think not? That's only because you might be thinking I must mean the noise of sound. Yes, that is one kind of noise. We live in a noisy world anyway, don't we?

However, here are some ways we make it even louder.

We talk all the time. We all know people like this. What they say they have already said—repeatedly. It is always the same discussion. It often contains some form of a phrase that points to the faults of others, rehashes the bad breaks of the past, and laments the unfairness of the world. Talking too much, without listening to others, or ourselves, is a very easy place to hide.

We hide in the noise of clutter. Even the most orderly of us have clutter. We all keep things that don't work, clothes we don't wear, objects we don't like, and stuff we don't need. However, some of us stack those things up so much that we can't think straight at all. Clutter drains us.

We lose things, and we have no space. We pay money to store things away that we never look at, but remain within our lives taking up room, and making noise. The noise of clutter is a fabulous place to hide from ourselves, and others.

The noise of busyness is the disease of our era. How busy can we keep ourselves? If we aren't making ourselves busy, we let others do it to us. To add insult to injury, we often use things in that busyness that make lots of noise.

I used to live where lawns were at a premium, and then I moved to where huge lawns are standard issue. Lawns are noisy. Lawn mowers and leaf blowers are noisy in loudness and time.

I am in full agreement with this quote by William Henry Hudson: *I am not a lover of lawns. Rather would I see daisies*

in their thousands, ground ivy, hawkweed, and even the hated
plantain with tall stems, and dandelions with splendid flowers
and fairy down, than the too-well-tended lawn.

Imagine the stillness of lawns planted as fields. Imagine
sitting quietly in nature just listening to the silence. That
isn't as farfetched as it seems. However, first we have to ask
ourselves, "Am I hiding in noise," and if we are, begin the
process of eliminating it.

Practice sitting quietly in active meditation. Listen within
to the still small voice, and then take action on what you hear.
Pause, Observe, Listen, and take action.

In the *Preface* we talked about the symbol of pulling the drill
out to clear the sawdust. This is the same as using the Pause,
Observe, Listen (POL) tool. Within a pause we can easily let
go of what is no longer needed, making it possible to continue
drilling down through habitual habits.

HIDING IN BUSYNESS

Let's talk more about busyness, because not only does it
often create a lot of noise in which we can hide, busyness all
by itself is a wonderful hiding ground.

In an age when things were supposed to be easier, and we
would have more leisure time, the opposite has occurred. "I'm
too busy," is a phrase we all have said to keep from doing
something we want to do. In busyness we don't have to think
too much or make radical changes, because we are too busy.

Try taking an hour off, without electronic interruption, and
spend that time quietly with your thoughts. As they occur,

watch them go by like clouds. Don't hold on to them or judge them, just watch them go by.

Listen within, listen without, and listen to the silent rhythm of the universe.

Feel yourself melding with the rhythm of where you are, whether it is in a chair or outside in nature. Feel the non-busyness, yet profound living of life that is always going on. Listen to who you are, listen to your heart's desire, listen to the still small voice within guiding you to living your life fully. In this hour off, notice that the world did not end because you were not rushing around making things happen.

Make this time off a spiritually healthy habit.

My husband has always taken quiet time the first thing in the morning. He sits in the dark, drinking his morning drink, and listens. And then we sit together and do the same thing. As you make this time off a habit, take more time away from being busy. Eliminate those things you are doing because you felt you had to, but actually they have nothing to do with you.

The interesting part of no longer hiding in the busyness is you will find that you are actually more productive. What needs to be done gets done with more ease and grace, and as you stop hiding, your life expands. That expansion takes place within the context of your preference of how you wish to live your life. Most of us do not desire to jet-set around the world, or to be famous enough to be known as we walk down the street.

However, even if you do find yourself that well known, that is still no excuse to hide in the busyness. Whether our days are simple, or complicated, we can still learn not to hide in the busyness of life.

Did you know we are trained to be busy so we won't think too much? Our schools were first designed to keep us in line with the religious beliefs of the Puritans. Their premise was that we are all sinners, especially the children.

Because many of the first settlers in America were English, much of our education system is patterned on the systems they brought with them. The Puritans, strict fundamentalist Protestants, believed education was necessary in order to read the Bible so that one could receive salvation.

This was in line with the beliefs of the Protestant Reformers. Schools made no distinction between religious and secular life. They inspired children to endure the hardships of a life in the New World through religious devotion.

The first compulsory education laws were passed in Massachusetts from 1642-1648. They were specifically oriented towards a segment of the population (non-Puritan) that was not, in their view, providing their children with a proper education.

Religious leaders were concerned about the rapid growth of the non-Puritan population and took these steps to maintain Puritan religious beliefs. The first act, called the Massachusetts Act of 1642, made education a state responsibility. Although the schools were not yet funded or required, education itself was, and all children were supposed to learn how to read and write, or parents would risk loss of the custody of their children. This law was amended and strengthened in 1648.

Children from poorer households received a minimal education, and slaves from Africa only learned what was necessary to attend to their masters. Later, during the industrial revolution, schools focused on teaching us how to sit still and follow directions so that we could be good factory workers.

Today the educational system is often too focused on passing tests, and only a lucky few learn how to think, and reason.

Perhaps if we don't think too much, we won't question the workings of governments, or the injustices brought about by just a few people, because they are keeping all the rest of us too busy.

Therefore, even if you think that you can't afford to stop hiding in busyness, do it for the rest of humanity.

Imagine a world filled with thinkers and imaginaries, and we were one of them. How many of us would then agree to the world's many inhumane practices, including wars, that we now let slide by, because we are too busy hiding?

Not Listening

We all know someone who literally can't hear, and chooses not to wear a hearing aid some, or all, of the time.

What a great way to hide. Not knowing what is being said, we can pretend that there is nothing for us to do, or to know.

Of course not wearing a hearing aid is obvious, but what about just not listening? When someone is talking, are we planning what we are going to say next?

Or perhaps we are not listening at all. Instead, we may be designing our home, thinking about our next date, or work, or our vacation—all wonderful hiding mechanisms for not listening when someone else is talking.

We don't listen to the signs of our lives, or we don't read the instructions, or we don't read what is written to us—the ways of not listening are numerous, and we are guilty of all of them at one time or another.

When we recognize them as a hiding technique, we have begun the real process of listening. We will start listening to what are we being told, and in the process discover that there is much to hear, either through literal words, or through signs and symbols. The more skilled we get at listening, the less likely we will answer "yes" to the question, "Are You Hiding."

CHECKING IN ON OTHERS

If you can see your path laid out in front of you step by step, you know it's not your path. Your own path you make with every step you take. That's why it's your path.—Joseph Campbell

Checking on others is a great way to hide. It is widely accepted, and it may even make you look like a good person. This is the one where you notice, react to, and try to do something about, someone else in hiding, lying, waiting or running.

We can easily see someone else's faults, and unwise habits. We can make a living at doing so.

In fact, there are professions where this skill of noticing is required and many a hider, liar, runner, and waiter has done a good job of hiding within their ranks.

Whew! You may be thinking, she means a profession like psychology, and that eliminates me.

Not so fast.

How about professions like teacher, mother, police officer, actor, father, banker, salesperson, coach, life guide—yes this list could include all of us.

If in our daily life we spend time observing others in order be good at what we do, then this is an easy place to hide.

The most dangerous way to hide in the checking-in-on-others scenario is by being a friend. In the name of friendship, we can point out others' faults, and consider it a demonstration of being a good friend.

Here is the key question to ask ourselves to keep us on track. Are we using these professions, and skills to hide ourselves?

We must be observant, wise, and aware. Leaving ourselves out of the observations, or observing ourselves as hiding but doing nothing about our own habits, is a habit that will someday boomerang back to us in ways we usually don't see coming. It's back to perception again. What we see in others is actually going on within our own perception.

We will become better at every profession we are a part of, if we begin with the correct premise about ourselves and others. We are not superior to others just because we see their faults.

It's a fact that we can't see what we don't already know. This works both ways. We can't see good unless we learn to look for and support good, and we can't see the "error" in others if it is not already something we have experienced ourselves.

Control and Planning

When I do good, I feel good; when I do bad, I feel bad. That's my religion. —-Abraham Lincoln

We know who we are, don't we? If I say, "control freak" raise your hand if it sounds familiar. I understand. I am giving up controlling and controlled planning myself, so I understand that it is a hard thing to walk away from.

However, once we begin to understand how miserable it is to always have to be in control, and to have everything planned, we can finally begin to give it up.

It certainly doesn't fit into the idea that God is the only cause and creator, or follow the guidance of "not my will but Thy will be done." Instead, it is the perfect place to hide.

There are many ways to control. There are those who feel as if they have no control over anything, so they take control over something that they feel they can do, like eating. Or perhaps control over others.

Some people plan everything so much that the joy of discovery and unfolding is lost in the details of getting it right. There is nothing wrong with being good at managing, or planning—in fact it is a delightful and necessary skill. However, only if it is based in the right premise; the premise that we are the action of the Divine, not a lone operator.

It's easy to spot controllers and controlled planners who are not only controlling and planning their own lives, but other lives as well. They always have to run the show, they change what other people have set up because it doesn't match what they want, and they punish others, in a variety of ways, for not going along with their plans.

None of us want to live that way. Let's give it up, and step out from behind the control curtain and get to know ourselves.

A tree doesn't control; it grows and shares itself, blessing all that get to know it.

One morning I woke up with these words ringing in my ears as if someone had spoken them to me. "Don't plan; share." I pass this idea on to you. It has helped me immensely in seeing the difference between controlling, and being, the action of Love.

HIDING IN THE STORY

Hiding in our story is very handy for many of us, because we have collected great stories. They give us wonderful excuses for our current behavior.

They usually begin with, "When I was," and continue on about life as it was when we were younger, how our parents treated us, what school was like, how our friends behaved—the list is endless.

Some of these stories are not so bad, and some of us have absolutely horrible stories to tell. Either way, when we use these stories to hide in and away from our current life, we keep ourselves away from living the blessings that life is offering us here and now. On the other hand, it is possible to use these stories to learn about ourselves and move on into life with a brave, and open, heart.

If you think you are stuck with your stories, think again. Go back and read the section on Right Thinking in this book. It will help reset that story in your memory so that it takes its proper place. I am using the idea of story on purpose. It is a story, and nothing more, and only occurs and occurred within our own perception of it.

Now is the time to talk about accepting guilt and responsibility for our stories, and then hiding in that pain. Why do we do this? Because we think that we, or another, created it and caused it. This is not true.

Please know that we do not create the situation or story line from our actions, or our thoughts—either from our current life, or from what some people call karma. Remember, there is only one cause and creator, and It tells only one story. That story is about unfolding and expanding good, equally, for every one of Its ideas. There is no one left out of, or separated from, all that is good. Because God, Good, is omnipresent, that is not possible.

Therefore, the story, or stories, that appear to be in and about your life are misunderstood events. Yes, they may have happened. Yes, they were either lovely, or horrible, or somewhere in between.

However, no story actually happened within big R Reality, the Reality of God, Good, who knew—and knows—nothing about it. Therefore, our True Being, our essential eternal identity, does not know anything about it either. Nothing has removed us from the Good that is God.

When we dream, we see many stories, yet we wake up from the dream, knowing that it was a dream. We often learn from those dreams, but we don't live from those dreams. What appears as our everyday life is the same as those dreams. As we wake up into the awareness of our true being, then the dream of human life and worldview begins to fade, and will correct itself based on our new awareness.

We are all aware of the illusion of dreaming. We don't wake up from a dream and then base the rest of our day or our lives on it. Perhaps we will look for the symbols found within the dream in order to become more aware of what we are thinking and perceiving, but it will not become the basis of all our actions. The stories found within our lives are nothing more than stories, like dreams. And like dreams, the stories and the story teller are one.

What we perceive to be reality magnifies. Magnify the story, continue to give it full power, and yes—it is a great place in which to hide.

However, I ask, "Why stay there?" Wake up! The big R Reality holds more possibilities than we can possibly imagine—all of them good—and everything will get better and better the more awake we become.

Hiding In Victimhood

Yes, I could have put this under the heading of Hiding In The Story because being a victim begins by believing a story.

However, it deserved its own category because we all do it almost automatically, at least once in awhile. Oh, I know, we all know someone who really plays up the victim story, but when we look closely at our own lives, we are doing it too.

There are many ways to hide in victimhood, but the one that has us sacrificing for others so we can remain a victim is particularly unlovely. In this one, we claim to be acting out of love for others, but in reality, we place a burden on them. They, of course, could then use this scenario to choose to hide in victimhood themselves.

We are not required to sacrifice the essence of ourselves, our desires, and our hopes so that others can have theirs. Many of us do give up a dream, or two, or three, so that our children can have theirs; or we work at jobs that may not be our first choice so that the family can be fed. This does not have to be chosen as a sacrifice; and most certainly we must not choose to act the victim in these cases.

If we do so, we have negated all that we have done for others; we have made them responsible for our unhappiness. Instead, we can lean back into the provision of Love. We can choose to do these things with delight, happy to have the chance to serve, which is not sacrifice. Instead of burdening others with our victimhood, we release them to live free of the guilt of our sacrificing for them. Guilt is a terrible burden to pass on to anyone.

It is easy to give to others so that we don't have to give to ourselves, but this is hiding. Be sure that what you are choosing to do is not based on victimhood.

You will find that there is a more elegant, and marvelous, idea for you to choose from for your life. Infinite Love does not take from one to give to another. Take action from this premise, and watch life unfold perfectly for you and the ones you love.

Another way to hide in victimhood is hiding in ill health. This is not a discussion of whether ill health is real or not. We are going to stay away from that issue for now. Instead, let's look at using ill health to get the attention we crave.

It could be ill health in terms of a disease or an injury. When we take the time to examine our motives for giving power to either of these situations, we will often find that they provide the perfect motive for not participating and for getting something we desire—from attention to income.

We have all probably tried the "I'm not feeling well" gambit to get out of going to school, but that habit remains into adulthood unless we become aware of it, and send it packing.

Here's a personal example of battling with the temptation to give in to victimhood, in this case an injury.

It was a beautiful day so I decided to walk longer, and explore a new way home. The ice had melted on the streets—or so I thought—so I had removed the chains on my shoes (yes, they exist and yes, they work) and I was happily striding down a new side street enjoying the view of the lake.

Suddenly I felt myself falling sideways. I hit the street with a huge thud as I fell directly on my entire side. As soon as I hit the ground, I got back up because I knew that it would not be wise to succumb to the belief of falling.

That was the easy part. Then the war began.

I knew that if I could hold to a Spiritual Perception that I—in God's image and likeness—had never fallen and if I could choose not be tempted into believing in what the senses were telling me, the result would be "no result" from the illusion of a fall.

I imagined how wonderful it would be to have direct proof that everything is only thought, and to know without doubt that maintaining a Spiritual Perception, and letting go of anything unlike Love, would immediately dissolve any negative situation.

That liar, which does not want us to know who we are, didn't let me alone for a second. It reminded me that I had fallen very hard and was lucky not to have broken something.

It told me I would be sore, unable to move my shoulder and hip, and that the bruising would be extensive. It suggested that I could "use" the injury to get a bit more attention from anyone, anywhere. It would give me something to say to people that they could commiserate with. I could fit in.

It was a war between what I knew to be True and the temptation to believe the worldview and what it was saying to me about who I was, and what had happened.

The barrage of tempting thoughts continued for days.

The fall was no different than any other event that tempts us to use the negative to achieve a positive, to succumb to something we know is not true, just to get a bit of love, or attention; to give into the idea of lack in any form, to accept the lie of separateness from Divine Love in whatever way it decides to make its appearance.

It is still the same lie.

What defeats this lie? Always the same Truth; there is only One, and it is Spiritual, and we are Its Being.

The result of the fall was "no result," and "no result" is what we want from any lie. Let's all resist the temptation to be part of the worldview so that we can fit in. This is not where we want to fit anyway. What we really want is to become aware of, and experience, Divine Love's infinite Oneness. In this Oneness, we always fit in.

It's much easier to give up material things, and pleasures, than it is to give up material worldview habits and thoughts, but imagine the result of giving up the habit of hiding in victimhood.

WHAT AND WHERE IS SELF-LOVE?

There are many paths to enlightenment. Be sure to take one with a heart. —Lao Tzu

Recently I started thinking about the idea of self-love. I begin wondering what the difference is between the self-love we want, and the self-love we don't want. Because on the one hand we hear we should learn to love ourselves, yet on the other hand we hear that self-love is selfish. It turns out, the word self-love can mean the exact opposite depending on who is saying it, and how it is used.

My mentor used to say this to me, "Self-love is more opaque than a solid body."* I often thought, "huh" when she said it, and decided she must not be talking about me, since I was so often down on myself. Where was my self-love?

Yet, looking back, I know she was trying to tell me something about myself. Now I see that being down on myself was the negative version of self-love. I was often attempting to find something I needed, by giving to others, so I could have what I thought I lacked. It was still really all about me.

That is what the negative self-love is about; it is "all about me." It rests in the human personality, and ego of self, and not surprisingly, it does not ever bring permanent happiness.

I wasn't trying to make life all about me. I was trying to be a good wife, mother, daughter, employee, and service provider. I was trying to do the right thing, all the time. However, because I didn't understand that loving myself meant not loving the human personality self, but loving the qualities of God present as me, I was often in need. This meant that without realizing it, life was often all about me.

Do we need self-love? Absolutely, but which kind? Jesus' admonition to "love thy neighbor as thyself" states clearly that we had better love ourselves well if we are going to treat our neighbors well too. This is tricky, I know. Same phrase, entirely different meanings, and entirely different results.

Perhaps the first step to seeing the difference between the two kinds of self-love is to begin with the question, "What premise is our self-love based upon?"

Is it self-love beginning with the premise of a human personality and needs—where we take care of ourselves through will power, positive thinking, control, destructive behavior (which is actually inverted control and will power), and hard work?

Or is it self-love beginning with the premise that we are the presence of Infinite Intelligent Love, which eliminates need of all kinds?

With the second form of self-love, we love ourselves because we are the reflection and expression, of God.

We observe the qualities of God that we uniquely express, and cherish their presence as us. We care for ourselves within the context of caring for the gift that we are to each other.

As knowledge of ourselves as the qualities of divine Love increases, so does our self-love. This is an easy love to have. This self-love removes ego. It eliminates fear. It dissolves being stuck in negative descriptions of ourselves. We learn to love, and treasure, the qualities we express. We give thanks for who we are. We find life flows from this kind of love, and we no longer need to use any form of human control.

It's easy to tell which self-love we are practicing.

In the human version of self-love, we experience need. We have all experienced this kind of self-love need. It is a need for anything we feel we don't have—from love, money, health, or time. Needing is not a good experience, or feeling.

Within Divine self-love there is no need, there is only the experience in each moment of the qualities of who we are, present and being lived as us. In Divine self-love, we find plenty of everything, and our love for ourselves flows to our neighbors equally without effort.

In human self-love we ask, "Notice me, help me, give to me, and take care of me." In Divine self-love the I Am is present. Within this self-love our personality and ego step aside so that we can be seen as we are—the reflection and expression of God.

Self-love within a spiritual context is a marvelous way to live. Opaque means not being able to see through something. Through the lens of human self-love we are unable to see the Truth of any situation.

However, as we are willing to know ourselves as the qualities of God, the opaqueness fades, and in the resulting clarity, we find our freedom from need. We experience instead the joy of divine self-love, which is always overflowing, filling our lives full of blessings without measure.

* Mary Baker Eddy—*Science And Health With Key To The Scriptures*

HIDING IN THE PAST

It is not life and wealth and power that enslave men, but the cleaving to life and wealth and power.—Buddha

Let's consider what we believe is the past, and family history, past and present.

At a family gathering a few years ago, we shared our favorite family memories. For some it was easy, for others, not so much. In fact, when I asked Del if he had a favorite family vacation memory (since that was mostly what everyone picked) he didn't have one; not only because he doesn't have good family memories, but also because his family never, ever took a vacation.

However, if you ask any of his children, they have a multitude of favorite family memories. I know, because they share them all the time.

We can either take our past and learn from it, or be buried in it.

As we traveled that week through family history, it was easy to see the frozen attitudes; stuck states of mind, and points of views. Not just in others, but in myself. The first night at our family gathering, I didn't sleep at all, because I was caught up in the same feelings and emotions that haunted my childhood—self-loathing and depression because I had felt misunderstood and disliked.

And even though many years had gone by, and much shifting, the intensity of the experience reminded me of how that felt, and it took some doing to shift away from that so I could let go, and enjoy the trip—which I surely did!

Yet, we must do more than just shift from bad memories to good ones, or let slide those things we don't like and embrace the ones we do. We have to let it all go. Our family history must all be re-seen as God in action, as shared love, as the unfolding of grace—with not one trace of ownership or heredity.

As we look at family, past and present, let's see what is actually present and let go of our self-will and justification—both on the good side and the bad side. It's all in the small r reality room, where everything is seen as material and measurable.

We can step out of that room to the Spiritual Perception of family, and consciously experience ourselves as the unique essence of Light that we are. We can embrace what appears as family members not as limited editions of themselves, but as a unique essence of Light.

FLOW LIKE FIRE

During one of our early morning talks in the dark, with our favorite morning drinks, we sat watching the fire in our stove.

The fire was doing something we had never seen before. It would quiet down so that all that we saw were very hot logs, and then a spurt or whiff of fire would rise and immediately blink out, as the entire roof of the stove would suddenly be alive with flame. Within moments, it would quiet down and repeat the process, but never the same way twice.

Fire is like that, it is never the same way twice; and yet the essence of it is always the same. Everyone knows fire when they see it, even though it has an infinite variety of ways to express itself. This made me think of plans and making lists.

Yes, I know that on the surface it appears to be a strange connection.

However, just a moment before we had been talking about plans and lists, and the fire's show that morning was the perfect symbol of the difference between how we think things should be, and how it is when we are aware of how life flows.

I thought, "What if we were more like fire when we made plans and lists?" What if instead of saying this is exactly how my day, my work, my party, my dinner, my life— my anything—is going to go, what if instead we accepted that the essence of our plans will always be perfect, and then let the outcome be expressed in a variety of interesting, and beautiful ways.

What if we flowed like fire?

Then instead of feeling remorse, or guilt, or anger, or emotion of any kind when our plans do not go as we expect, or when we don't finish our to-do lists, what if we flowed like fire and lived within the awareness of the beauty and uniqueness of each moment?

What if instead of seeing ourselves as limited humans, we saw ourselves as a unique expression of divine Mind? Then no matter what happens, we would be aware of our innate, individual perfection of being.

When we study fire, it is easy to see that no matter what shape it takes, it remains fire. We can see the same thing with anything in nature. A tree remains a tree, and a squirrel remains a squirrel.

It is when we get to ourselves that we often stop having this basic awareness. We think if we haven't done this or that, or the situation we are in is not as we planned, that we ourselves have been affected adversely and become someone else.

However, the Truth is, we remain who we have been and always will be. Even if we don't know who we are, it doesn't change who we are. As we let go of expectations, fears, and judgments, the view of ourselves begins to clear up. When that happens, we may think that we have changed, but we haven't.

Instead, we have begun to see the face of our own fire—the Truth of our being.

In his excellent book, *The War of Art*, Stephen Pressfield makes the point that we must always be about our work. Yes, we must. Just as fire must be doing fire, we must be doing who we are. However, if we make the mistake of measuring that idea in human, linear, and stilted terms, we miss the fact that when we are aware of the essence of ourselves, like the fire, whatever we are doing, we are still doing "our work."

I love making lists and plans. I have a list by my computer I check every hour. I have plans for today and plans for next year. However, if my plans change in either the next moment, or the next month, it will not change who I am. And if I don't let emotions cloud my awareness, it will not change the quality of my day, or of my life.

As we strip off expectations and judgments, and discover the infinite ways that we express the essence of our being, we discover that we have always been an individual expression of the Divine Mind.

We are like the fire. The only real plan of fire is to be fire. Like fire, we flow into and as our life, in an infinite variety of ways, while always remaining ourselves. We will become increasingly aware of this fact when we let joy be our guide, and allow gratitude to light our flame. Then our lives become what they are—a spectacular show of infinite expression. Never the same, always beautiful.

7

— · —

CHAPTER SEVEN

*N**ever, never be afraid to do what is right, especially if the well-being of a person or animal is at stake.*—Martin Luther King

It's easy to tell when we are lying. At least it is easy when we are paying attention. It's easy because of the way it feels. Only those who don't know they are lying, either through innocence, or through depravity, don't feel the result of lying.

Of course, all lies begin within ourselves and to ourselves, and if we get too good at lying to ourselves the consequences are very dangerous.

Therefore, when we ask ourselves, "Am I Lying?" we mean not just to others, but first, "Am I lying to myself?" Sometimes it may be justified to lie to another, if the moral law of protection dictates it, but most of the time it is best to tell the truth.

However, lying to ourselves is always a dangerous and slippery slope. I first saw the results, and dangers of lying to oneself in a childhood friend. When we were young, everyone in school knew that his dad was going out with other women, and even young girls, because he was cruelly blatant about it.

However, my friend's mom pretended that it wasn't happening, which of course affected her life. It was worse for my friend. As he got older, he refused to speak about it. He would even say that it wasn't true. I watched as that lie ate him up and consumed the boy that he was, and hid it from view. He started acting like his dad, and lying to himself, and others, about it. Because he knew that he and his dad were wrong, and he couldn't face the truth, he started closing himself off. In time, he became bitter and angry, and acting in ways he once would have hated.

I can easily look back and see that if he had just been willing to admit there was a problem with his dad, and worked through that problem for himself, none of the rest of what followed was likely to have happen.

He is not alone in this behavior. We all lie sometimes to ourselves and to others to protect our ego, or because we don't think we can survive telling the truth. Sometimes we don't call it lying, we might call it exaggeration, but it is still a lie. Unless we pay very close attention to what we say, it is easy to fall into this trap.

Our human ego is always playing a game of one-upmanship, because it believes that doing so is necessary for survival.

Because we are, in big R Reality, a reflection of God, we can defeat this habit by first setting our premise to our right identity, and then as we notice the lies, either big or small, we can choose to correct them. As we dissolve and eliminate habits like these, because we are basing our behavior on the true essence of ourselves and others, there is another lie that will often show itself. This is the lie that it is necessary to heap guilt and judgment upon ourselves for what we have done.

Although it is always necessary to notice, and then eliminate behavior that does not reflect our True nature, it is not necessary to punish ourselves once that behavior is gone. We don't punish our children in their teens for what they did when they were two. This same kindness, and clarity, needs to be extended to ourselves. If we do not do so, it will cloud our view of the goodness of God, and of our own spiritual identity.

I said it was easy to tell when we are lying. It is. When we refuse to look at the facts, when we rationalize our behavior, when we are angry, and judgmental, or depressed, there is a lie waiting to be exposed.

Yes, exposing our lies to ourselves is painful, but not nearly as painful as losing our loved ones, and ourselves.

When we lie to ourselves it is inevitable that in some form, we will lose ourselves, and those we love.

TELLING THE TRUTH

We do not need magic to change the world, we carry all the power we need inside ourselves already: we have the power to imagine better. —J. K. Rowling

Of course, the opposite of lying is telling the truth. Obvious isn't it? Or is it?

Most of us feel that if we don't say anything we are not lying. Perhaps. However, we are also not telling the truth either, and that is the point of the question, "Am I Lying" after all.

The Twelve Step Program of Alcoholics Anonymous deals with this issue of lying in a few of their Twelve Steps—let's look at two of them.

> Step Ten, states: "Continued to take a personal inventory and when we were wrong promptly admitted it."

This requires a constant monitoring of the internal lying that goes on in all of us, and then demands that instead of festering a lie, the truth must be told.

> Step Five states: "Admitted to God, to ourselves, and to another human being the exact nature of our wrongs."

This is a crucial step in this process. We can tell ourselves that if we know the truth it doesn't matter if anyone else knows it. This step demands that we say it aloud, that we fully face our fears. Why do this? It is certainly not to embrace our fears, but to release us from the prison of lying.

The poet and scientist Piet Hein wrote:

The noble art of losing face

May one day save the human race
And turn into eternal merit
What weaker minds would call disgrace.

Our fear is that if we tell others what we have done wrong, or admit to the mess we think we have made, we will lose either our friends, our loved ones, our reputation, and our pride, or maybe all of these, all at one time.

However, not one of these is as valuable as losing our soul, or the essence of our being.

For what is a man profited, if he shall gain the whole world, and lose his own soul? Or what shall a man give in exchange for his soul?—Bible, Matt: 16:26

The glorious part of telling the truth is the reward. One woman in our *Shift* community wrote about how many wonderful opportunities were flooding into her life as a direct result of telling the truth about a situation, and taking action on what she discovered; opportunities that she could never have expected, or tried to make happen.

She said, "I just want to say that this has really all opened up since I dared to share with you all the traumas I was experiencing post house sale. Just letting you all in on my deep secret of possible short sale/bankruptcy/whatever on the house has seemingly opened the floodgates. Yesterday I saw a branch of the bank and said a little prayer of gratitude as I was waiting to cross the road!"

It is a lie that says to us that we will lose our friends, our loved ones, our reputation, and our pride. Instead we regain our pride, find our true friends and loved ones, and rebuild our reputation as someone who can admit what is happening, and work through and out of it.

MAKE IT APPROPRIATE

Telling the truth to both ourselves and to a trusted friend, or advisor, is different from releasing information over everyone and requiring them to bear the burden of our truth telling. Choose wisely to whom you share.

And for heaven's sake, don't be one of those people, who after deciding that they might as well tell the truth, start spilling out details to everyone. This is a good way to hide from the feelings, and a wonderful way to run from the responsibility.

Actually, it is another form of lying; thinking that spilling your guts to anyone who will listen is actually truth telling. Once again, lying is going on.

I once wrote a truthful letter to two people I love, and instead of destroying it after writing it, I sent it. Although the letter did speak the truth, as I personally saw it to be, it was my self-indulgence that wanted them to know about it.

I look back now and wonder, "What did I want to come of that letter," because there was absolutely nothing positive that the letter could, or would have, ever done for them. Instead, it caused a riff that although long ago forgotten, and forgiven, by them, remains a point of sorrow for me, because I know how painful it was for them to receive that letter. I caused it by telling the truth inappropriately, and only as I saw it, and not as it was for them.

SELF-AWARENESS TESTS

Each of us is an integral idea of infinite Mind. This means that it takes all of us, expressing our Unique Spiritual Blessing, to be the full completeness of the I Am.—Beca Lewis

I often have people I work with take a test, or two, designed to help them understand both their life preferences and the way they make decisions.

It helps me understand them better, but most of all it helps them understand themselves better, and enables them to design the life they really want to live; not the one that someone else wants, or wanted, for them.

Since this request has the outcome of freeing them from hidden habits, and false beliefs, about themselves, it is always interesting to note that everyone, me included, feels like lying on the test.

Why? Because as we stare at the questions, there is an underlying theme going on within ourselves. It says something like this:"If I choose this answer it probably means I am a certain kind of person and I don't want to be that kind of person."

Once again, this lying is to ourselves about ourselves. No one else ever really needs to know what we wrote on the test. The glory of this knowledge is, if we really find out who we are, we can choose to be that without the walls and limitations built up to protect a false belief.

Why would we think one kind of person is better than another? It is those pesky perceptions again, brought on by words spoken directly to us about ourselves, or ones we have read.

For example, the first time I took one of those personality tests and I turned out to be a D. I was horrified when I read what that meant. All I could see were the negative words; "Bossy, demanding, unthinking, driven."

I wanted to be soft, lovable, and helpful. I couldn't see how I could be that D person and also be soft, lovable, and helpful.

So I would try to lie on the tests. However, really I was always lying to myself, and that made it worse. Because, when I was not aware of who I was, I did act very bossy, demanding , unthinking, and driven.

Once I accepted that a D had a profile I could embrace, and consciously chose to use these qualities (that untamed, and untrained could appear negatively) I was able to behave more as my heart desired—soft, lovable, and helpful. I embraced, and applied the positive aspects of a D, dissolving the negative ones.

No individual is better than another. In Truth, we are all the qualities of God, and so these tests are not defining our limitations, but displaying our unique strengths. We are all unique ideas and individualities of the divine One, the Principle of Love. Instead of lying about who we are, we embrace it. Experience the joy of living as yourself, without the lies, and without the deception.

Choosing

We often lie to ourselves, and others, when we make choices. One way we can tell if we are lying is to ask ourselves if we are rationalizing.

The funny thing about rationalizing is that it can argue on both sides of the same issue. Thinking choices through can make it appear as if both sides of the choice are good sides, so how can we come to a choice that is in our best interest?

We can start with our intent. First, we begin with the big intent, the intent of our life, and then keep bringing it down to the choice itself.

Choices following the still small voice within often feel like the harder choice. However, in the end, it is the easier one. Sometimes when we make a choice, we feel relief. This is because we have chosen the path of least resistance, and we are not really heading down the road of our true intention.

Asking ourselves constantly, "Am I Lying," and then being willing to hear the answer, will solve most of our choice problems. Of course, we lie the most to ourselves, and then come up with a good reason why we have made that choice to those that are affected by it.

The good news is, we can always change our mind, and usually must, in order to end up where we mean to be going.

I watched a video clip of New Orleans Saints quarterback Drew Brees throw a football at a target. He threw ten times, and ten times hit the center of the target. However, when the film is slowed down it shows the ball nose making subtle corrections the entire trip to the target.

Another example we all know is that of the bumblebee who flies to its destination by making hundreds of directional switches. Like the bee, and the ball, we can easily re-choose if we keep our eye on where we intend to be going.

THE ART OF PERCEPTION

The spiritual life is a call to action. But it is a call to action without any selfish attachment to the results. — Eknath Easwaran

I love this idea. That Life Itself is a call to action. However, there are two pitfalls that often cause us to fail at this idea, and do the opposite and take no action. Not the action of conscious non-action, but no-action.

The first pitfall is that as humans we think we know better than infinite Life Itself. The second pitfall is that we think we are human, and as such we are co-creators, and creators.

Taking action without being attached to the outcome is a science and an art. It is a scientific fact that there is no intelligence in matter and the only intelligence is in Infinite Mind. Physicists have proven this fact, although they are often reluctant to call it Mind, as in Spirit.

The art of it comes into play as we attempt to live what appears as a human life while knowing that we aren't human, we are the idea of God.

This surely is an art, isn't it? Isn't this a portion of what Henry David Thoreau meant when he said, *It is something to be able to paint a particular picture, or to carve a statue, and so to make a few objects beautiful; but it is far more glorious to carve and paint the very atmosphere and medium through which we look. To affect the quality of the day—that is the highest of arts.*

It is this part of the quote—*to carve and paint the very atmosphere and medium through which we look*—that carries with it a significant message, because it is a statement about perception.

If we begin with the perception that we are a human, creator of our life, well, we all know the amount of pressure and stress that results from this point of view. It is inescapable. No matter how many pressure, and stress reduction techniques we learn, they will only damp down the underlying fear that this point of view produces. How can we affect the quality of our day, if we have not been an artist with our own perception?

Choosing the perception of a human, it may appear that it is possible, with a lot of work and a bit of luck, that we can create a life that we love.

Choosing the perception that we are Life Living Itself, we experience an immeasurable difference.

One carries with it stress; the other releases us to the freedom of living as our USB, our Unique Spiritual Blessing.

Our thinking does not create the life we experience. It is our perception about life that makes up our experience of it. This is a subtle difference in statement, but it makes a huge difference in the outcome. One produces many emotions, and drama, much stress, and guilt, or complete denial. The other brings relief, because we know that what may appear one way is only that way because we are seeing it that way, through our habits and the lens of our perception.

We can shift our perception in every moment, and affect the quality of our day. We can be an artist with our perception, and in any moment choose the highest understanding we have about the fact that all that is ever going on is "Life Living Itself and Love Loving Itself." Imagine that. Just imagine what this means!

I implemented this type of shift of perception as we searched for a home, and went through the process of buying one. Most of the time, I was able to stay within the point of view and state of mind using "I Am" statements. I said statements like, "I Am Home Itself, and therefore there is no need to worry about this outcome or try to make it happen."

Sometimes, I could feel the fear and stress rush in, and the lies would tell me it would never work.

Then, when it looked as if it was going to work, I still had to stay in the "I Am Home" perception, or the fear of, "Oh my gosh, what have we gotten ourselves into" would rush in.

That human habit of lies is always waiting at the door of our mind. It may hide in the bushes, but it is there, and at the first crack in the doorway, it will push its way in and try to settle into every corner of our consciousness.

Nevertheless, it can be removed immediately by a perception shift, and Truth can fill the spaces of our consciousness so there is no room for fear to sit down or hang out.

To be an artist of perception takes practice, just as being an artist of any kind takes practice. However, one day we will all witness that the artist is actually Love, Life, Mind, Soul, Spirit, Principle, Truth—Living and Loving Itself—and that we are the consequences of that action.

Action is the movement of the spiritual essence we call God. Therefore, action is what we are, too. It's easy to allow ourselves to take action when we know that even though the outcome is not ours to decide, it will be better than we imagined.

WHEN LYING SOUNDS SO TRUE

Here is a story I have never fully shared before. I have told bits and pieces to one person, or another, but never the whole story to anyone. I am willing to tell this now, because it will make clear the point I want to make, because it is imperative for us all to know the lie that sounds so true.

I used to be terrible at picking romantic relationships, but this was one of the worst of all.

It started right after a divorce. A friendly divorce, but still a divorce. However, I was not unhappy. In fact, my daughters and I had moved to a beautiful townhouse with a very affordable rent. We were the first ones to occupy this townhouse, as it had just been built, and my income was "luckily" low enough to qualify for a low-income housing rate.

It was an adjustment. I had to sell my house, move the girls to a new school district, and I was sleeping in the living room, and on the balcony, in order to let them have their own bedrooms. I was happy doing so. I was surrounded by new and felt free for the first time in ages. Sleeping on the balcony in California felt like a gift, and not a sentence.

Then I started dating a man I knew from a business connection. I was smart at first. Instead of having him pick me up, I met him when we went dancing, and came home alone, happy as a clam.

However, he appeared to offer me something I hadn't realized I always wanted: A business partnership as part of the relationship. I realized that I wanted to speak, write, and teach with someone who thought, and believed, the same as I did.

He had all the right words. He was a part-time minister after all. He appeared to have the right connections and right ideas, and I was tempted.

However, once when he came to pick me up at a dance class, as I saw him approach I heard a small quiet voice ask, "Why are you dating a wolf?" I ignored the message, because I wanted what he was offering. So I let him into my life more and more. Soon I lost my perspective, and I was hooked into his lies.

We started going to conferences, and events, together. He knew how to ham up our relationship there so everyone would talk about it. I didn't notice I was paying for it all, because it appeared to be what I had always wanted. In retrospect, I see it as a dangerous counterfeit.

After a few months, he said we had a job in Hawaii. I had put on my wish list a trip to Hawaii, a trip to Hawaii paid by someone else, just months before I met him.

"Wow," I thought. "It is coming true." I had the enough presence of mind to ask my mentor what she thought.

However, at the time she was coming from the same erroneous belief system, as I, so we discussed that it was too bad women needed a man to get ahead in the business world, but since we did, why not take this leap?

I went to Hawaii with him. We worked, but not really together, because instead of being partners, he kept me out of the loop. He asked me to marry him, and I accepted. Looking back, it was ridiculous because I was not happy at all. I had not yet discovered that just because something on our wish-list comes true, doesn't mean it is because of Love. This too was a dangerous counterfeit.

My two daughters were living alone in our beautiful townhouse, and I missed them terribly. However, the pull of that dream and his lies were keeping me locked into that counterfeit situation. I came back home to pack. I spent four days packing his house, and mine, and putting them in storage. I shipped my car to Hawaii. I paid for everything.

When I look back at this time, guilt and regret really tries to kick in. My daughters were alone. One went off to college, and the other went to live with her dad. That lasted a very short time. The older daughter had to come get her, and move her to a friend's family who took her in.

Finally, I realized that his entire goal was to keep me unhappy and needing him. Awareness started to break through. Yes, I wonder too, "What was I thinking?" I wasn't.

I was lying to myself the same way he was lying to me. How do I know? I rationalized everything.

One day I was speaking to my mentor on the phone. She knew only a tiny bit of what was happening, but she did know that I wasn't happy. She asked to speak to the man. He gladly said "yes" and proceeded to give her his charm act. She asked to speak to me. As soon as he handed me the phone she said, "Leave now!"

I trusted her. We had both been wrong, and I knew I needed to follow her advice. I gathered the people we were working with and laid out why the venture they were planning would never work. Effectively I closed the business.

The partners were grateful. He was not. I was offered a week away at a retreat on a nearby island by a friend, which I gratefully accepted.

After that week, I left Hawaii with much less than I had brought with me. I carried a suitcase small enough for me to put in the airport locker. I spent the rest of the day walking on the beach, waiting for the plane to leave. I had spent all the money I had earned from our home sale, so I had to leave all my possessions in Hawaii, including my car. My children were living elsewhere, and I had nowhere to go. All that I had left was in my suitcase.

A friend picked me up from the airport and took me home, and let me sleep for days. Another friend offered me a small rental she owned that had just opened up, and I moved in.

Another friend paid my bills for two months until I could think again. Another friend called and gave me a job. Many years later when I was trying to understand what love really acts like, I remembered this time and saw clearly the truth in the statement, "Love always shows up."

I started writing, and I went on a talk show and exposed him, but not to himself. I discovered that the entire time I was living with him, he was carrying on a long-distance relationship with his girlfriend that he had supposedly given up when we met.

All of this because I believed that someone—a man—outside myself could give me what I yearned to be. He was lying, and I was lying, to myself first, and then to everyone else in the situation. Notice that in spite of all these mistakes, I was never abandoned. My true friends were always there and cared for me. Love remained. I just had to step into Its flow, and accept Its gifts.

How could all of this have happened in the first place? I had **not** set a clear intent about love and relationships. I certainly was not coming from the correct premise about partnerships, love, or family. Because I did not do that, I was always vulnerable to an idea that was almost right, but not based on truth.

Many, many people are smooth-tongued liars. They know all the right words, they have all the right answers. Pay attention. Make sure that you don't become one yourself, because you have lied to yourself first.

Never allow someone to be your priority while allowing yourself to be their option. —Kelly Angard

Sing—Knowing You Have Wings

For as long as I can remember, one of my favorite poems has been Victor Hugo's poem, *Be like the bird that, passing on her flight awhile on boughs too slight, feels them give way beneath her, and yet sings, knowing that she hath wings.*

Isn't this poem beautiful? It sings about the principle, and the perception, that no matter what appears to be happening, when we know who we are, we can sing, knowing that we have wings, and knowing we can easily fly up, and away, to safety.

Once, while walking in the woods, I watched a hawk's nest high in the tree, swaying in the wind, and felt the meaning of this poem even more deeply.

Having felt for myself the bite of fear while sitting high in a tree while it swayed, I thought of what it would feel like to be that high and ride through the blasts of wind that whip the tree limbs around so freely.

I imagined that if it were me, I would worry that the limb would break, and then what would I do?

And then I laughed out loud, startling a few wood creatures I am sure, with the realization of what the *knowing that she hath wings* means to a bird. If the limb would break, they would simply fly away, singing as they always do, with the joy of the freedom of flight.

Notice that my thought about falling began with a *what if* question that made me feel afraid. Of course I would be afraid I could fall, if I didn't find peace in the knowledge that there is always safety, and always a solution, and this knowing will act as wings, always flying me to freedom and safety.

Victor Hugo's life's work was profoundly influenced by his awareness of the social injustice, inequality, suffering, and uprising that was the underlying theme of France in the 1800's, the place and time in which he lived. His writings, like *Les Miserables*, were directed at pointing out, and bringing to light, what was wrong within the system, so it could be corrected.

Yet, he wrote a simple, and elegant, poem on how to escape, without harm, the mess that the worldview dualist system makes. He wrote about how the bird, faced with a weak and falling branch, sings, knowing that she hath wings.

Not only does she fly away as the weak branch breaks, she sings. She sings **before** the need to fly. She sings in the morning in celebration of a new day. She sings in the day, not because she must, but because she can.

A Chinese proverb says, *A bird does not sing because it has an answer. It sings because it has a song.*

Are you singing your song? Until we are all aware of, and acting within,the awareness of the oneness of what appears as mankind—aware that we are within the circle of One, and not without it—aware and acting from the Principle of the Infinite Intelligence known as Love—social injustice, inequality, and suffering will appear within the times we live. Yet, we do not have to be part of the suffering, we can sing, knowing that we have wings. We can sing as the bird does, because we have a song.

No matter what we call the voice of the system— worldview, predator, devil, or monkey mind—this voice is belligerent and loud, but subtle. It demands that we listen to it. It brings with it all the emotions that begin, and end, with fear and its tag-along friends called doubt, anger, discouragement, frustration, sadness, despair, and the rest of these life-hope-stealing companions of the what if negative voice.

Since we do live in a thought Universe, we must be able to recognize who is asking the what if question, and who is doing the thinking. It's hard to sing when we are within the grips of the what if voice of fear. However, there is another what if voice, and it sings the song of the Infinite Principle of Love.

The still small voice within brings gifts of love, with its corresponding comforting feelings of hope, encouragement, possibility, joy, and the rest of its friends that encourage us to sing, knowing that we have wings.

Sometimes this comforting voice also says *what if*, but the *what if* it asks is not loaded with fear, it is loaded with hope and possibilities. It sings to us that there is always an open door—there is always a solution—we are never separate from the gifts of Love. There is no one who has more than another within the Infinite provision, and equality, of the Divine.

To hear this voice we must pause and listen to the stillness within the peace of Love. To hear this voice we have to stop agreeing with the what if voice of fear. It may still be making noise, but we are giving up the habit of listening to it, because we have the thought-wings of awareness of the omnipresence of Love.

What isn't love is loud and insistent that we pay attention to it, like a petulant child, or a bully, or even a terrorist.

That doesn't mean we bow down to it and give in to its demand to be afraid. Instead, we pay attention to the peace, beauty, and love that is all around us, when we do this, what to do about the bully of fear becomes evident.

If we attempt to fight fear, it has us in its grip.

Instead, we sing knowing that we have wings, and rise above it, watching it dissolve itself as it battles with itself, which is all that it knows how to do.

Sing, knowing that you have wings, sing with celebration, sing with gratitude. Share your song, sing of joy, sing of good, sing of the evident abundance in your life. Sing, because singing of these things reveals even more goodness. Sing because it dissolves the blinders imposed by fear, and reveals the consistent care always present for you.

Sing of the abundance of your neighbors and friends, show it to them, and share it with them. We cannot be rich without all being aware of their richness.

Are you afraid that your clients can't afford you, or your employment can't keep you working? Sing, knowing that your clients have wings too, sing knowing that abundance does not come from people, places, and things, but appears because we are present, because we are the representation, and idea, of abundance itself.

Keep singing when the wind blows, or if the limb you are on begins to break. Sing, that there is nothing to fear, because we are One within the One of the I Am.

Gather your thoughts to this place and keep them there. Let the illusion that threatens dissolve itself into the nothingness from which it came, never touching you, or your loved ones.

8

— ◦ —

Chapter Eight

Every one of us has said, "Yes, I am Waiting, Yes, I am Running, Yes, I am Hiding, and Yes, I am Lying," some of the time. We are all uncovering unwanted habits. The point is to dissolve them as quickly as possible into spiritually healthy habits.

Sometimes it is very simple to do this. Asking these questions, and answering them truthfully, brings awareness, and awareness often does the dissolving without any extra work on our part. If we would keep asking these questions all day, every day, many issues that have clogged up our lives would simply dissolve away.

Instead of living life with a bag over our head, or our head stuck in the sand—either one of which leaves us completely vulnerable since everyone else can see and we can't—we are at least observing our life. This means we are more likely to do something other than wait, run, hide, and lie.

Sometimes we have to do more than become aware. Sometimes we have work to do, and actions to take. Which returns us to the idea of perception—point of view, and state of mind. Since *what we perceive to be reality magnifies* then it seems entirely logical, and very wise, to choose the most abundant, joyful, infinite perception possible.

This actually is easy to do. The idea that there is a Divine Principle of Love that is omnipresent, omnipotent, omniscient, and therefore omniaction, is a cornerstone of much of the world's agreement. It is certainly mine.

Who wouldn't want the outcome of living from that perception?

I really think the answer is, nobody. The only reason it is not consciously chosen by everyone is we doubt that there is such a Divine Intelligence. However, for the moment, it doesn't matter whether there is or not, because it is perception that determines our own personal reality, so why not choose this one?

Of course, there are the pundits who will say that this is not a fact. "Prove it wrong then," I suggest.

See if you can prove that what you *perceive to be reality* does not magnify. In the meantime, while they waste their time, you are asking yourself these questions and you are choosing to stay awake, alert, and aware. In doing so, you will experience it for yourself.

I therefore suggest, for your own sake, that you try this experiment. Choose the best perception you are willing to accept as true, and let it lead you into a better life.

However, just choosing a better perception, or the Infinite One, as your *point of view perception*, will not actually move much of your life into what you desire.

The culprit is the second half of the perception rule, our *state of mind perception*. Sadly, it is our state of mind that we are most unaware of, and what must be addressed in order for things to change for the better.

We can choose a wonderful *point of view perception* like, "There is only Love." However, if our *state of mind perception* says something like this: "I know that's not actually true, and I can prove it because I don't feel loved or loving, and bad things always happen to me. Besides, what is so loving about what goes on in the world," then this *state of mind perception* diminishes, and sometimes completely negates, our *point of view perception*.

If our *point of view perception* is that the Infinite is Abundant, and yet our state of mind perception is in fear and doubt, it is hard to see the Truth, that yes, the Infinite is Abundant.

So what do we do? We have to shift both our state of mind, and our point of view, and bring them into harmony with each other.

This takes us back to *The Four Essential Questions*. When we answer, "Yes, I am hiding," then we begin the process of shifting. One way we can do this is to use a logical progression of thinking. It might go something like this, "I notice I am hiding, but since Love is omnipresent I can never hide from Love. Since the Truth of my being is that I am the expression of Love, then this hiding is a lie about myself."

As we state this kind of Truth, the fear that is causing the hiding begins to fade away. Is it this simple? Yes, and no.

Yes, it is this simple in concept. No, because we are so locked into our own prison of beliefs that escaping them can sometimes be daunting. However, if we are willing to let them go, it gets easier and easier.

I often ask people, "What is stopping you from living happily, and freely, abundant?" Often that answer is, "I doubt myself."

We can easily see that this doubt is a state of mind and a point of view all rolled into one.

Doubt and discouragement are the devil's tools.

They are easy to use because we are so willing to pick them up and claim them as our own. It seems right. After all, we can all say to ourselves, "Look at what I can't do, or what I have done, that never worked out."

The question is, "Do you want to live in that state of mind and point of view? How badly do you want to escape the outcome that this perception produces?"

No one can escape your perception for you. In fact we are all too busy escaping our own. We can help, support, guide, and walk together, and we can celebrate the shift of perceptions together, but we can't do it for you.

You have to decide. Once you do, the solution is easy. **Shift your perception, and keep it there**. Seriously. That's it.

Yes, I always write about shifting perception. How could I not when that is the answer? Do you want me to make up a false solution just to bring about another useless theory that distracts, and disrupts, the world?

There are many false solutions. If you are not yet ready to move out of the prison of human beliefs, you can surely find a *point of view perception*, and *state of mind perception*, that matches the quality of life you want to live.

Or instead, you could believe all the stories based on a human viewpoint that make life sound more exciting. Stories are good. I love a good story, but that doesn't mean I want to *live* in it.

Eventually, we will all find that stories are not freeing us from the real illusion—that we are human.

If not human, then what are we? We are idea of the One Infinite Mind.

I am fully aware that this makes no sense to a human point of view. Neither does the fact that the earth goes around the sun, or that railroad tracks don't converge in the distance.

Again, it doesn't matter if you believe the point of view that we are all the ideas of the One Infinite Mind in order to experience the outcome of shifting to this point of view.

Let's return to *The Four Essential Questions*. Yes, this is the ultimate use for them; to shift perceptions. As we notice that we are waiting, running, hiding, and lying, we also notice the point of view and state of mind that has produced this response. Then we have the chance to make a conscious choice to choose another perception, and let that shift cause a change in our behavior.

The worst thing that could happen is that your life will get better. The best thing, well heck I don't know, because the Infinite One-and-Only Creator is surely in charge of that, and for that fact I say, "Thank God."

ASK, IS IT TRUE?

We have answered, "Yes I am lying, or hiding, or running, or waiting." Now what? Add this next question, which is actually a two-part question. We are going to ask, "Is it true, lower case t," and then ask, "Is it True, upper case T."

Here's the difference.

Asking, "Is this true," lower case, is asking within the context of what our five senses know. Is it true that no one has ever been kind to you, loved you, or helped you? Absolutely not. Someone somewhere has done all those things for each of us. There is nothing true about any absolute statement within the small r reality, or everyday life.

Because we know that shifting perceptions changes everything, asking this one question, and then listening for, and accepting, the answer, can change everything. Just asking any of these questions, and then continuing on our day as if nothing happened, isn't useful at all. Ask the question, then Pause, Observe, and Listen.

Often this means that we will have to give up cherished reasons for believing what we do, and behaving how we do. Here's a question to ask yourself, "Which one do I most want? To be right, or to be happy?"

Once we make the decision to be happy, and all that happiness entails, it is time to move on to the second way to ask that question. Asking, "Is this True," upper case, means we are asking is it True within big R Reality.

Big R Reality is the Reality that the One Divine Mind is, and knows. We are not talking about the god that is human like, that doles out punishment and knows about bad. We are talking about the spiritual idea of God that is all there is, and is only good, so therefore only knows, Good.

Does this God, or It, the Principle of Life, know about any of our actions within the small r reality? No. For some people this is a huge disappointment, because they think this means they are not personally loved or cared for, and that their prayers are not heard.

True, those prayers are not answered in the conventional sense. However, when we pray, it begins our alignment with the omniscient One, and this process will reset our perception to the Truth of our being, bringing us back to the Big R Reality.

Yes, we are personally cared for in the same way we care for ourselves, God cares for us, because we are the reflection and idea of God.

How To "Snap Out Of It"

One grateful thought at a time, just like one snowflake at a time, changes the landscape. —Beca Lewis

Have you ever said to yourself, had it said to you, or said to another, "Just snap out of it!" This statement supposes that we have the ability, knowledge, and desire at that moment, to do so, but this is often not the case. Therefore, this little solution is dedicated to all of us for those times when "snapping out if it" sounds good, but feels impossible.

Of course, we all know that the first step in "snapping out if it" is wanting to. When we are deep in joylessness, discouragement, despair, or doubt we may feel abandoned in this state of mind. The question then is, "How do we become willing?"

Here are two quick ways to get over the *why bother* feeling and begin to be willing to "snap out of it" and be happy again.

> 1. Pause and remember a time you were happy.
> To remember might take some deep recalling and imagination.

Compare it to how you feel now. Really feel the difference. Were you more comfortable physically, and mentally, when you were happy?

Keep feeling the difference until you catch that glimmer of "willingness," and hold on to the feeling. Think of it as a tiny flame you have to keep alive.

> 2. Do it for someone else. In everyone's life, there is someone else, or a cause, that we love enough to choose to do something for them, if not for ourselves. Albert Einstein said, Only a life lived for others is worth living.

Be willing to snap out of it so you can "do" for someone or something else. (Not sacrifice ourselves for someone else—don't get confused here, these are two different things.)

3. The next step is easier than discouragement would want us to believe. It's the step of gratitude. Everyone knows that being grateful is the perfect "snap out of it" remedy. However, exactly how is that done?

Have you ever told yourself to be grateful and heard the answer, "No I don't want to!" Of course you have! Why would discouragement want you to leave it?

We are going to be grateful in spite of it! How are we going to do this? Repeat steps one, and two, if necessary and focus on that willingness flame. We are going to get it to burn brighter by blowing gratitude on it—but how, and for what?

Most of the time when we have fallen into a funk, it is not just one thing that has taken us there.

Usually, it is that one little extra thing that happens and we finally say, "I can't deal with it!" Uncovering all that has taken us down might take forever, and often keeps us there, as we ruminate over it like a cow chewing its cud.

Instead, let's begin with a premise, a point of view, that happiness is something we have a right to have, and that it is actually the by-product of the Divine Order of Good running the universe. Yes, in the funk we say, "Yea right," and that's okay. Let's prove it to ourselves anyway, because remember, it is more comfortable for everyone when we allow ourselves to be happy.

Here are a few examples of how to be grateful in a way that resets the internal system back to its original state of joy, and happiness.

In today's climate of uncertainty and change (which is always present, just more promoted now than it has ever been), it may appear even more difficult to step away from it. Don't believe it. Snapping out of it now is just the same as it was thousands of years ago, and as it will be in the future, because the lie is always the same. It's just that the story is told in a variety of ways.

Let's take one of the lie's variations that pops into everyone's mind when in a funk, and see what we can do with it. How about the thought, "Nothing I ever do makes a difference, and no one really cares anyway."

This thought, if true, would mean there is an aspect of the Divine Order that is not working right. This is impossible. Therefore, our perception shift will be to prove this fact to ourselves so that we can once again experience happiness.

To do this we will need to notice those things that do make a difference. Notice that when you smile at people it lights up their face. Notice the dew sitting on the grass makes it sparkle. Watch a baby smile, a bird sing in the tree, or the sun rise in the morning.

Avoid the thought that none of this is because of you, and instead translate what you are seeing back into qualities for which you can be grateful.

Perhaps it goes like this. "I am grateful that someone is happy, I am grateful for all those sparkles, I am grateful for the innocence of babies, I am grateful for birds singing, I am grateful that the sun always rises." Feel the Truth of this!

Keep going—the flame is starting to grow: "I am grateful for the order expressed in the stars moving smoothly in the night,

I am grateful for the beauty of a flower, I am grateful for the ability to see all the evidence of the Divine Order, of which I am an integral part."

Keep going—fan the flames with more gratitude for the power of Love. Become immersed in the feeling of it. "I am grateful that trees send down roots, for the bulbs that bloom in spring, and for the clouds that scuttle across the sky.

I am grateful for the presence of light in all its forms, for the laughter of children, and for the hugs of my friends."

As we fan this flame of willingness with gratitude, we will rise out of any state of mind that hides happiness from us. Translating things back into thoughts, or qualities, we find the spiritual joy that opens our eyes to the infinite power of Good, and Love, that is the ground of our being.

We are not required to swing between joy and sorrow. Within the Divine there is no shadow of turning; there is only the eternal now of ever-present Joy. Happiness is a by-product of this awareness, and we can always choose to return to it.

Next time you hear "snap out of it" you can say, "Okay, I know how to do that!" And you know what? Sometimes that statement is all it takes!

Be thankful for what you have; you'll end up having more. If you concentrate on what you don't have, you will never, ever have enough.—Oprah Winfrey

STUCK, INERTIA, AND THE FIRE WITHIN

Knowing trees, I understand the meaning of patience.
Knowing grass, I can appreciate persistence. —Hal Borland

We installed a wood burning stove in our living room that we use to heat our home. It works wonderfully well, and it continues to provide guidance as well as warmth. Watching it one morning, it demonstrated to me the difference between *inertia* and *stuck*—and how to dissolve both.

I never had a wood burning stove before. I thought that it would be just like a closed stove. However, a wood burning stove has an airtight glass door on it so you can see the flames. You can also feel the heat the same as a fireplace, but because of its design, the heat is not dispersed up the chimney, which makes it many times more efficient at heating.

This means that you can't just throw wood on the fire. You have to open the sealed door, which then allows the oxygen to flood into the fire. Therefore, you have to pause before fully opening the door so that the fire does not build too quickly from that rush of air.

One day it had warmed up outside so I hadn't put any new wood on the fire during the afternoon. That evening, as I prepared to build the fire again, it appeared that all that was left were a few very small embers. On this same day, I was thinking about the difference between inertia and stuck.

Because it appeared that there was no fire, I wasn't as cautious as usual when I opened the door. The moment I did so, the fire literally exploded into flame. "That," I thought, "Is what becoming unstuck looks like."

Like those embers, all it takes is the swift infusion of oxygen or, in our case, Truth, and what has been silently and steadily burning within will burst into bloom. It doesn't take much.

On the other hand, there is inertia. This can happen when we have let the fire go out completely. Then it takes a lot of small tinder, coaxing, and a build-up before the fire begins to burn efficiently again. That is what inertia looks like.

We often think of inertia as not moving. However, *inertia is either a state of rest, or a state of motion, that is resistant to change*. We see this in our everyday life in our habits. It is the way we have always done it, whether we are doing something, or just standing still.

To change our state of being, like the fire, takes an outside force proportional to how ingrained the habit has become. How dead the fire is beforehand determines how much force, or fuel and oxygen, is needed to start it burning efficiently again.

Approaching this from the right premise of Spiritual Perception, when we are in the state of mind of inertia, it will take more awareness and discipline of thought to change a bigger, or more ingrained, habit of thought than a smaller one.

On the other hand, when we are stuck, the desire and intent is already burning.

Then it takes just a small amount of outside force, or awareness of Truth flooding into our consciousness, to propel us out of stuck and into Life.

Of course, these two ideas are intertwined. Both states of mind, called stuck and inertia are misunderstood perceptions of the True nature of Life, which have become habits of thinking and acting. However, understanding the difference between the two may help relieve the frustration we sometimes feel when we have been steady students of Truth and yet it feels as if the fire of our life has not yet begun to burn efficiently.

There is great comfort and relief in knowing that the Infinite Principle never experiences inertia and never gets stuck. It is never even aware of our misperception. It is always operating in the harmony and perfection of graceful unfolding.

This means that as we add the fuel of awareness and perception, and diligently tend to the fire within, what appears as stuck or inertia will dissolve into nothingness. Either state does not exist in the perfection of the Truth of Being. As the mist dissolves, we will experience our current highest awareness of Love Loving Itself in practical ways, far beyond our human design and planning.

Open the door of your fire within, and let in the Truth of who you are. It doesn't make any difference whether this action explodes your life into bloom, or if you have to diligently build the fire first.

Sooner, or later, the **illusion** of stuck or inertia will dissolve, and the infinite abundance that is you, will stand revealed.

What Voice Is Yours?

Voice? What Voice? I always find it a bit alarming to know that there are people declared insane because they hear voices. It must be a matter of degree that makes the difference, because we all hear voices.

These voices come from many places, and the ones we listen to (perhaps this is the key in the insanity issue) determine the outcome in our lives. Therefore, it is imperative that we take the time to determine what's up with those voices.

I'll cover three types of voices.

The first one is *outside voices*. This should be the easy one. We can all tell when an outside voice is speaking to us, can't we? We should all be very capable of deciding whether those voices have our best interests at heart.

We should be good at it, but often we are terrible at recognizing that many of those voices are only for, and about, themselves and that they intentionally spread the disease of fear.

You know those outside voices; they can appear as our friends, family, and the media.

Even those voices that perhaps mean us well, are often not the best voice for us to listen to. It is too easy for us to forget that we don't have to believe what an outside voice is telling us. Often, instead of thinking it through, we assume that because they say so, it must be true, and therefore it must be true for us too. Therefore, we accept an outside voice, and what it is saying as true, and as if it were our own voice. It's not.

The second type of voice is the *voice in our head*. We all know this one very well, because it is constantly speaking. What we may not be aware of is that the voice in our head is always, always, always—yes, always, putting us down in some way. We are never good enough, we never have enough, and we are always doing something wrong. We are stupid, or lazy, or a combination of every negative quality possible.

If that voice were an outside voice, most of us with any sense at all, would not only not listen, but never allow it in our lives again.

Not so with this voice in our head, because this is the voice that we **think** is our own voice, speaking to ourselves. After all, it speaks in our language, talks as we do, uses terms we understand, and we can see that it has a point. Nevertheless, this is not true.

This is not our voice. It is the liar's voice disguised to sound like our own.

Its lies are built on a teeny-tiny piece of what we feel is true, so we decide the whole thing must be true, and of course, since it sounds like our voice, we think we have to listen.

Listen to me now.

Here I am, an outside voice that not only has your best interest at heart, but also knows the Truth about you, and wants you to know it too. That voice inside your head is **not** your voice! No! Not ever!

This means you can stop listening to it, you can stop paying attention, you can stop letting it ruin, and run, your life. I am not saying it will stop talking, because it won't. However, you will learn not to hear it, and the volume will be turned so low you will sometimes forget that it is there.

The only way to get to that peaceful place is to begin now to say to it, "I know you are lying, I know you are not my voice. I know you don't care about me at all. I know your intention is to keep me from living a full and productive life. So from this moment on, you are on your own."

You may have to repeat this many times before you— not it—get the message, but for the sake of your permanent freedom, don't give up.

Now for the *good voice.*

Yes there is a good one. You know this one too, but if you have been listening to all the other ones, you may be out of practice in hearing it.

The other voices may be so loud that you have to really work at hearing this good voice.

The only way to hear this voice is to be quiet. It is that still small voice within.

This is the voice that guides you gently and with care and kindness. This voice is direct from your Self, the real self. This is your voice, because it is from the One, the eternal divine essence of Love.

You can trust this voice. This is the voice that says, "The real you has never done anything wrong. You are the loved of Love. You are the action of intelligence." This voice speaks the Truth.

Listen to it, follow its guidance, and all will be well.

FACE AND REPLACE

Don't wait for the last judgment. It takes place every day.—Camus

Here you go—a technique to use for shifting perception that works everywhere, anytime, and gets easier with practice. Face and Replace is so simple children can do it. In fact, they are better at it than most of us adults.

Remember, *what we perceive to be reality magnifies*, so whatever we are perceiving to be reality becomes more and more real to us.

Our senses do not create reality; they report to us what we believe it to be. Good and faithful servants, they tell us exactly what we expect, and often want, to hear.

One morning two things happened to me that demonstrated quite clearly the idea of being aware of what is going on.

I was preparing to do an exercise program that involved putting in a video, and following along with it on my exercise machine. I turned on the TV, and inserted the disc. Before I could switch over to the exercise program I was caught up in an infomercial for skin care. Although I clearly know all the manipulation tricks used, I was still intrigued. I sat at the edge of the bed, and watched, thinking how wonderful it would be, if what they were saying were true.

I left the DVD in the open tray, and went to my computer to check out the product. If I hadn't already set the habit of *pause before buying*, I would have ordered the very inexpensive trial offer even though I knew it meant I would be on a monthly installment plan for more. But, I didn't. Instead, I decided to Pause, Observe, and Listen, and I headed back to exercise.

All was well for about thirty minutes. Then I got tired, and bored. Having done this program many times, I started thinking about what was coming next instead of just being present.

I managed to keep my focus for a few more minutes when, without thinking, I turned it off.

Even though in that moment I unconsciously shut off the program, I knew that I was not quitting for good. I knew I would return. Why? Because I knew that it is only a false belief about myself that sometimes stops me in the moment. However, because of my underlying intent to express myself in movement, I will continue to return to it.

The problem arises when we take those momentary "I don't want to" messages as a truth to follow, when they are actually very much like the manipulation of an infomercial—in reverse perhaps. It stops us from doing something, rather than getting us to buy something.

Here's how *Face and Replace* worked for me in this instance. I faced the fact that I wanted to buy that product to fix my wrinkles. I replaced that desire with a simple pause. I paused to listen within to see if this was the right choice for me. There was nothing esoteric about it at all. Just a simple stop and listen. In this case, I got a very clear awareness that it wasn't the right thing for me to do.

In the second instance, I faced the fact that I was tired and bored, realized that in that state I had stopped the process. Instead of blaming myself, and feeling guilty, I simply replaced those ideas with the statement that I would return, and then trusted myself that I would.

I have a third example. A few minor events occurred one day that for some reason took me to the panic room. You know the one where it starts to feel as if you don't know anything, you can't do anything right, you are totally misunderstood, and all your work will never pay off because you can't do it right, ever—I could go on and on, as I am sure you could too.

It was as if a robber had broken into my home (my consciousness) and was stealing my peace, and happiness.

When I found myself in that room, I immediately closed the door behind me, to keep the robber out. Of course that meant that the robber was still waiting for me outside the door. I knew that eventually I would have to come out of the panic room and face what was terrifying me.

I knew there was no real danger, because it was my thought that was causing the panic, and that it could be stopped in the same way. Therefore, I faced each incident that was bringing on the fear, and replaced it with Truth. In this case, it was the Truth of a Spiritual Perception.

It went something like this.

First, I became aware of the fact that all my fear stemmed from an outside point of view. I was trying to make something happen in the world, on the outside, and I was getting outside feedback.

The next step was not to run from what I was hearing, or from the emotions it brought with it, but to look it squarely in the face and let it know that I "saw" it.

Then, instead of fighting where it wanted me to fight, or run away, I chose my own arena.

I went to the room, into the state of mind perception, where all the wonderful Truths I have learned are housed, and I pulled them out, one by one. Within myself, I faced each outside lie, and said in effect, "You can't scare me because you have no power."

Yes, I went back to the fact that omnipresent Love does not contain fear, or sorrow, or lack. Therefore, the fact that all of those appeared to exist for me was just an illusion. A very vivid illusion, but still an illusion.

Maintaining the *point of view perception* that Love Loving Itself was all that was really going on, meant I also had to bring my emotions into check, or my *state of mind perception* into harmony with that *point of view perception*.

I went for a walk, I read a book, I listened to words of wisdom, I breathed in a quiet space, I watched the birds outside my window, I stepped outside and smelled the air and I did a few stretches—all the while maintaining the best point of view that I could. Eventually the panic was dissolved, and I returned to my work.

Sometimes *Face and Replace* takes a split second; other times it take minutes, or hours, and sometimes days. Nevertheless, Love, Truth, God, always carries the day, because It is the only power. The other power is a lie that only needs to be exposed and replaced with the Truth. No matter what lie it appears to be telling, it is actually only ever telling the one lie: that there is an absence of Good, Truth, or God.

THE BIG MELT

Where we live, in the winter, snow covers the ground most of the time. As spring approaches, I wait with anticipation for the emergence of green shoots that I know are preparing themselves beneath the snow. However, in order to see those shoots the snow must melt.

Every day, I look out my window to see how much more land has been revealed. In the same way, our coverings must also melt to reveal what is sprouting beneath. As we let go of running, hiding, waiting, and lying, the beauty of our lives, and or our unique self, is open for us to experience, and for all to see and appreciate.

As snow melts, it provides necessary water for the plants beneath, but it does not feel pain in the process. As our icy coverings melt, we do not need to experience pain either.

We can allow what we have learned to feed, and sustain, what is emerging.

Visible As Myself

As we let go of all the evasion tactics, and we find a blissful rest in the assurance that Good, God, is all there is, then the Unique Spiritual Blessing that we are begins to emerge, and our life begins to reflect our true spiritual nature.

It is glorious to wake up, even a tiny bit, to the concept that what we consider a human, a person, is in Reality God seeing Itself. We are reflecting God, divine Mind, Love, Truth, Life, Spirit, Soul, and Principle and It is saying, "Here I Am, Visible As Myself."

Today you are You, that is truer than true.
There is no one alive who is Youer than You.—Dr. Seuss

— • —

AUTHOR NOTE

Thank you for reading my books! It is for you that I write.

If you like what I write, you can help spread the word, and keep my work going, by "liking" my books where the option is offered. I would be honored if you would also post your honest reviews of the book. This will help other readers decide whether it is worth their reading time.

In today's world it is the reader that spreads the word about books they like. If you like mine, anyway you choose to spread the word will be so helpful and appreciated. I thank you in advance for all that you do!

I hope this book has helped you discover more about the Truth of yourself, and that your life will expand in wonderful ways because of this knowledge.

Join my mailing list at becalewis.com and choose your free book.

I am looking forward to getting to know you! ~ *Beca*

— · —

OTHER PLACES TO FIND BECA

- Facebook: facebook.com/becalewiscreative

- Instagram: instagram.com/becalewis

- Twitter: twitter.com/becalewis

- LinkedIn: linkedin.com/in/becalewis

- Youtube: www.youtube.com/c/becalewis

ALSO BY BECA

The Ruby Sisters Series: Women's Lit, Friendship
A Last Gift, After All This Time, And Then She
Remembered, As If It Was Real...

Stories From Doveland: Magical Realism, Friendship
Karass, Pragma, Jatismar, Exousia, Stemma, Paragnosis,
In-Between, Missing, Out Of Nowhere

The Return To Erda Series: Fantasy
Shatterskin, Deadsweep, Abbadon, The Experiment

The Chronicles of Thamon: Fantasy
Banished, Betrayed, Discovered, Wren's Story

The Shift Series: Spiritual Self-Help
Living in Grace: The Shift to Spiritual Perception
The Daily Shift: Daily Lessons From Love To Money
The 4 Essential Questions: Choosing Spiritually Healthy
Habits

BECA LEWIS

The 28 Day Shift To Wealth: A Daily Prosperity Plan
The Intent Course: Say Yes To What Moves You
Imagination Mastery: A Workbook For Shifting Your Reality
Right Thinking: A Thoughtful System for Healing
Perception Mastery: Seven Steps To Lasting Change
Blooming Your Life: How To Experience Consistent
Happiness

Perception Parables: Very short stories
Love's Silent Sweet Secret: A Fable About Love
Golden Chains And Silver Cords: A Fable About Letting Go

Advice:
A Woman's ABC's of Life: Lessons in Love, Life, and Career
from Those Who Learned The Hard Way
The Daily Nudge(s): So When Did You First Notice

ABOUT BECA

Beca writes books she hopes will change people's perceptions of themselves and the world, and open possibilities to things and ideas that are waiting to be seen and experienced.

At sixteen, Beca founded her own dance studio. Later, she received a Master's Degree in Dance in Choreography from UCLA and founded the Harbinger Dance Theatre, a multimedia dance company, while continuing to run her dance school.

After graduating—to better support her three children—Beca switched to the sales field, where she worked as an employee and independent contractor to many industries, excelling in each while perfecting and teaching her Shift System® and writing books.

She joined the financial industry in 1983 and became an Associate Vice President of Investments at a major stock brokerage firm, and was a licensed Certified Financial Planner for over twenty years.

This diversity, along with a variety of life challenges, helped fuel the desire to share what she's learned by writing and speaking, hoping it will make a difference in other people's lives.

Beca grew up in State College, PA, with the dream of becoming a dancer and then a writer. She carried that dream forward as she fulfilled a childhood wish by moving to Southern California in 1968. Beca told her family she would never move back to the cold.

After living there for thirty-one years, she met her husband Delbert Lee Piper, Sr., at a retreat in Virginia, and everything changed. They decided to find a place they could call their own, which sent them off traveling around the United States. They lived and worked in a few different places before returning to live in the cold once again near Del's family in a small town in Northeast Ohio, not too far from State College.

When not working and teaching together, they love to visit and play with their combined family of eight children and five grandchildren, read, study, do yoga or taiji, feed birds, and work in their garden.

Printed in Great Britain
by Amazon